For Corliss, in absentia

# Discover your
# MASTER
# CHAKRA

## About the Author

Stephanie S. Larsen has been teaching students about the seven soul-rays and how to connect to God through them for eight years. She founded *Awakened By Stephanie* to help others evolve spiritually and become aware of their master chakra. Visit her online at www.AwakenedByStephanie.com.

## To Write to the Author

If you wish to contact the author or would like more information about this book, please write to the author in care of Llewellyn Worldwide, and we will forward your request. Both the author and publisher appreciate hearing from you and learning of your enjoyment of this book and how it has helped you. Llewellyn Worldwide cannot guarantee that every letter written to the author can be answered, but all will be forwarded. Please write to:

Stephanie S. Larsen
℅ Llewellyn Worldwide
2143 Wooddale Drive
Woodbury, MN 55125-2989

Please enclose a self-addressed stamped envelope for reply,
or $1.00 to cover costs. If outside the USA, enclose
an international postal reply coupon.

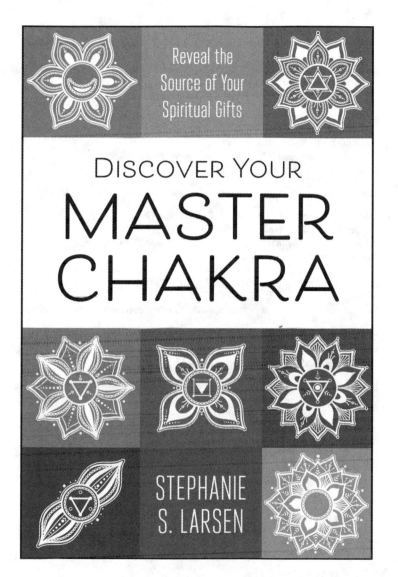

Reveal the
Source of Your
Spiritual Gifts

Discover Your

# MASTER
# CHAKRA

STEPHANIE
S. LARSEN

Llewellyn Worldwide
Woodbury, Minnesota

FIRST EDITION
First Printing, 2017

Book design by Bob Gaul
Chakra figure on page ix by Mary Ann Zapalac
Cover design by Lisa Novak

Llewellyn Publications is a registered trademark of Llewellyn Worldwide Ltd.

**Library of Congress Cataloging-in-Publication Data**
Names: Larsen, Stephanie S., author.
Title: Discover your master chakra: reveal the source of your spiritual
    gifts / by Stephanie S. Larsen.
Description: First Edition. | Woodbury: Llewellyn Worldwide, Ltd, 2017.
Identifiers: LCCN 2016047267 (print) | LCCN 2016052038 (ebook) | ISBN
    9780738749266 | ISBN 9780738751368 (ebook)
Subjects: LCSH: Chakras—Miscellanea. | Color—Psychic aspects. | Seven rays
    (Occultism)
Classification: LCC BF1442.C53 L37 2017 (print) | LCC BF1442.C53 (ebook) |
    DDC 131—dc23
LC record available at https://lccn.loc.gov/2016047267

Llewellyn Worldwide Ltd. does not participate in, endorse, or have any authority or responsibility concerning private business transactions between our authors and the public.

All mail addressed to the author is forwarded, but the publisher cannot, unless specifically instructed by the author, give out an address or phone number.

Any Internet references contained in this work are current at publication time, but the publisher cannot guarantee that a specific location will continue to be maintained. Please refer to the publisher's website for links to authors' websites and other sources.

Llewellyn Publications
A Division of Llewellyn Worldwide Ltd.
2143 Wooddale Drive
Woodbury, MN 55125-2989
www.llewellyn.com

Printed in the United States of America

# Contents

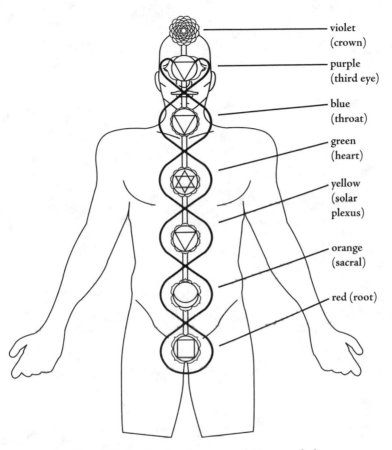

violet
(crown)

purple
(third eye)

blue
(throat)

green
(heart)

yellow
(solar
plexus)

orange
(sacral)

red (root)

*Figure illustrating the placement of the seven chakras.*

# Acknowledgments

I wish to thank both my parents, Rhonda and Steve, for giving me a work ethic and allowing me to think as I pleased when I was growing up. My father made it possible for me to write these words because he knew I could. He taught me the value of knowledge, including that which couldn't be externally verified in every respect and probably wouldn't be allowed in every space and time. My grandmother, Marvel, was a spiritual teacher in the art of compassion throughout her life, and it is her home that has shocked and awed so many of my clients with its extremely humane, grateful energy that never seems to stop.

Joseph Crane extended his prior knowledge of the seven spiritual gifts through his work with non-corporeal beings, including the one who led him and all who followed from a burning ship in the Tonkin Gulf during the Vietnam war. (You can read about that in *On the Wings of Heaven*.) Joe received his initial teachings on the master chakras from the great mind of Alexander Everett, New Age pioneer, who helped Joe listen to himself so he could respond back to such voices as the one that saved his life. Alexander studied all the religions of the world before teaching the seven spiritual gifts, known as soul-rays—one of many approaches to human evolution. This text is informed by Alexander's teachings to Joe, and Joe's direct teaching to me. Joe created the basic framework through which we understand the differences between the colors as we know them today. In this book, I have elaborated on Joe's basic content for a wider audience and done as much as possible to keep the information clear for beginners.

There were many others who helped me learn what these seven spiritual gifts were all about and how to impart them to others. Among them were Robbie Nicolai, who gave me the energy to become a spiritual advisor and trusted me with the highest of her teachings. Also, Heidi Shelton-Oliver helped me indefatigably grasp what each spiritual gift was all about, showed me how to figure out more about them, and corrected me when I was wrong. She helped me understand deeply all seven colors so I could teach them to others. It was a big job, and it took a long time and a lot of trial and error. Heidi is still with me.

Even though Alexander introduced one of the largest non-religious spiritual movements in the United States, and even though Joe teaches across the country in his Eden and Children of Life events, which you can join anytime, the fact that each one of us has a master chakra that is clearly recognizable remains one of the best kept secrets in spirituality.

My one-on-one clients, whom I've helped move forward in their lives since 2013, are responsible for monetarily supporting me while I was working on this book, and inspired it in the first place. Paula Hoerner is a stand-out client who is now a partner in this work. How I even started being a teacher-healer takes another book; it's a result of an improbable but incredible journey I went down with my teacher Dan Hanneman, who also taught me, Jill, and Tarek how to be healers.

Lastly, my fast friends and mastermind partners—Laurra Warneke and Jill Borsos, healers you can work with—have done countless things for me. They believe in the quality of my work as a writer, teacher, and healer. Each of them differently embodies the strength, support, compassion, and love of greens in their gifts.

# Introduction

Chakras are energy centers in the body. Knowledge of the chakra system comes from the Vedic culture of India, which has a long spiritual tradition, and the chakras have been a major part of the philosophy of life for people there. This philosophy has both a scientific aspect and what we consider to be a religious one. The chakra system alone is able to describe all the qualities of what it means to be a human being on the physical, mental, emotional, and spiritual levels. This is its power. I've spent years studying the different energy centers and how they function.

Here is a brief overview of the chakras themselves and how they progress, connecting the body, mind, and spirit:

*Red:* represents the physicality of things and the physical aspect of the world. The human body as it connects to the physical world.

**Orange:** the joy of expansion and creativity; the seat of sexuality.

**Yellow:** the finding of your identity, ego, and power in the human body.

**Green:** the place where the material and spiritual mix. You experience love and the unity of spirit and matter, God and humanity, in the same body.

**Blue:** where you speak what you've discovered about the world. Verbal self-expression and enlightenment's expression.

**Purple:** expression of truths in terms of beauty, visions from the mind's eye: art. Creation of relationships based on love.

**Violet:** when you've expressed art, you see everything as a whole community, continuous with yourself. You feel connected with Source and at peace and oneness with others. Expansion happens continually, like in the Big Bang. You serve.

Each master chakra has a separate chapter where I delineate its qualities and give examples of how it plays out in our daily life, especially through our relationships. Relationships are often the place where we learn about ourselves the most. A master chakra is the primary energy that guides and defines who we are, and furthermore, understanding our master chakra can be one of our greatest tools for directing our energies in the best way for our advancement.

Think of the chakras as each having their own deck of playing cards with all the various suits and numbers, or ways to unfold experience in life. Those chakras can also be represented by people with certain gifts, or areas of giftedness, on the talent side of the equation. On the shadow side, or dark side, most people carry a certain master chakra—their anger tells me they are a blue, for example. Or, their analytical nature tells me they are a yellow—not a one but a ten, since they also give orders, but not like a red. Alternatively, if someone is actively creating a new vision for others to follow, I call them a red ace, or a leader who is a step ahead, not just carrying out someone else's work. Do you see how it works? A person's master chakra will shine through everything they do, for better or worse. You can use your gift more or less, and you can be in your gifts or your traps. You can focus from your color or pretend to be someone you're not.

The chief desire of one's master chakra tends to structure the life purpose of that person. So, when we interact with someone as a king, queen, or other card, we do it from the point of view of our master chakra. We might be a yellow queen interacting with a blue two. If we are both schoolgirls, we might be twos, but different colors. If we are more powerful, more ingenious, more external in the way we live our life, we move up numbers and suits. But so often when we are drawn to another person, it is because they express their master chakra gift in ways that both defy our particular point of view and also keep in play expansion opportunities for us, whether we sit low or high in the deck. Because after all, what we desire in another person usually pertains to an expression of their primary gift, no matter what suit they are wearing. We need what they express on the rainbow to compliment the working out of our most current set of circumstances.

In time and space, we are born on a ray of light, born into a life purpose that lets us manage one chakra more than the rest—to create a dominant vibration within and without us. You might have anywhere from two to a thousand people in your life. It does not matter so much. The important thing to keep in mind when dealing with a person is how they tend to show up. So, the first purpose of this book is to answer the question: which colors are we dealing with? We can take the perspective that they spend a certain amount of time in the shadows and a certain amount of time in the light. They might function well or not at all. But are they using an emotional, mental, or physical point of view? Are they wearing a yellow, or green, number? What are their intentions? Are they working with others in their same level of power, like a queen working with a queen, or are they defying other suits? Are they acting alone? Can they be played out, dealt in, or given a rest? Why are they here, and where are they going next? Who unlocked the door to this, anyway? This Alice-in-Wonderland, no-man's-land world where no one seems to understand each other and nobody knows who's in charge?

If you think of this book like the dominant force in your card game, with the people in it you know, Alice's friends, you'll come to understand the true reality of how the game of life is often played, and played to break your heart unless you put it back together, piece by piece, into a whole because you believe in yourself. Because people use their strengths and their weaknesses both to gain their own sustenance and give it to others they love, we need to know what they are capable of. We also need to know ourselves and how we can increase divine order, instead of contributing to the shattered faces of this world, awash in chaos.

How the human dynamics game is played as it is on the level of soul rays can help you explore your own power in relationship to others. You'll glean some wisdom and no small measure of strength to proceed on your own terms. Also, you'll be able to be yourself more easily instead having to pretend to be a card or a color you're not. Finally, you learn, little by little, how to reconstitute harmony within yourself and your relationships.

A big reason I write things that only a handful of people yet know is because I have the blue spiritual gift for the duration of this lifetime, and as such, I can do no other than share my knowledge and understanding of each master chakra as it is progressed in me.

When I was in high school, and not long before I became a high school teacher, I was standing out next to the gas tanks on the farm where I was raised. I am not sure why I was standing there. No place was off-limits to me. This was the best place to get subliminal energy, as the fumes off-gassed into the realms. As I was looking at my energy in a subtle but not so subtle way, I entered a mode of understanding that was clearer than I usually experienced. I saw myself not only from above, but simultaneously from the side. I could see that I was masculine and I was feminine. In fact, the energy was really familiar to me, as I realized this is "me," across time. The energy was so familiar, it was more familiar than my own body or present personality. This is what people always give the label "weird," I thought. This is why I am called that. It is also why I was sometimes called "gay" by people who had no idea how to understand me.

I loved my gay friends, and I had had a best friend in sixth grade who was gay. But I was not gay myself. People seeing me as "gay" came from a place of judgment. The world judges people who are evenly balanced between masculine and feminine by pulling them down from the place where we are going as a species, which is a place of intensive investigation of the feminine side of things that actually balances the masculine point of view.

My ego and my mind—pulling the thoughts from the collective unconscious in order to give a meaning to what I was seeing—attempted to assist. Yet who was the real I? What was the pure energy that I saw? Was I who I thought I was, or was I the person "they" thought I was? Labels seemed inadequate to describe the truth.

Not two years later, in college, I took a computer-based personality test for Psychology 101. It was fall and I had just started school. The results came back a "0."—You are perfectly balanced between masculine and feminine, it said. You are androgynous. I looked to my left, I looked to my right. I hoped no one could see my results. Androgyny was a better, more accurate label. Yet I was still uncomfortable with that. Not being gay myself, it was easy to judge.

The first time I had heard an explanation of why I was masculine and feminine and still a girl was when I learned about the blue master chakra. In order for me to understand my feminine make-up, which also included a balance between masculine and feminine, I had to redefine the concepts I used to see myself and others. In order to become comfortable again, I needed different tools with which to prepare thought. I had to give myself a new concept of self, for how to see it and what to see. I was too unhappy with who I felt myself to be. Some of these ideas were received, but I was perpetuating them. In freedom and grace, instead of sadness, I had to change my vibration. I needed to wake up spiritually. And one big opportunity came when I was twenty-nine as I made my way forward, this time on the spiritual path.

With the help of my friend Heidi Shelton-Oliver, I learned how to perceive other people's spiritual gifts in my free time. My own spiritual gift came easily to me, but I would spend years observing other people's gifts in order to obtain a deep grasp of them. It was a long time before I could definitely identify a yellow or green. Today I have no trouble identifying a person's spiritual gift, and I do so without even thinking about it, often after talking to them only a few minutes. However, sometimes people can hide their color and the truth unfolds gradually.

This writing treats key characteristics exhibited by each master chakra and the concepts and philosophies they hold dear. It also illuminates key contexts, or arenas, in which each master chakra tends to wish to work and play, and generally be in the zone. Examples in each chapter are based on my personal observations of the people in my life. The purpose of figuring out your own master chakra is so that you can more thoroughly grasp who you are and how you work with others to achieve harmony and disharmony alike.

Feel free to open your mind to the awareness that you hold. I am not telling you something you do not know. I am bringing together the elements you already know into new categories so you can see people from a different, possibly more useful perspective. In this book, I open you up to a world you may not be aware of. It will take bravery to see the world in this way.

To begin, tell yourself you are ready to learn a new way of seeing other people. If you can do this, you can receive this system. This is my gift to you, the red, the yellow, the green, the orange, the purple, the blue, and the violet.

To receive the rainbow overhead into your heart, open your mind, your heart, and listen with your soul. Each chakra correlates with a color of the rainbow. Respecting that we can be anything we wish to be, we must first come to understand where it is we come from. You can enter this gate of enlightenment so you may see that all people are made in God's image and likeness and will hold forever the power to become any color of the rainbow they wish.

## How to Use this Book

The first thing to keep in mind when reading this book is that any reference to "God" references your own higher power.

This is a spiritual, not a religious, book, and its information can function as a way to unveil the beauty and the peace hiding inside any religion or spiritual path. Before turning to the chapters on each color, take time to read a short description of each master chakra. They appear before the quiz, a tool that helps you determine what your master chakra might be. After figuring out which one is yours, you can explore it more in the appropriate chapter. Each master chakra chapter is meant to stand alone. When reading through each color in succession, you can gain a good understanding of how each color is unique. To learn what colors your friends are, simply read through each chapter and ask yourself, "who do I know who seems to have this master chakra?" Once you can identify one person in your circle who has that color, it will be easier to add more. After the color workbooks, there is a list of key characteristics of each chakra that relates to body, mind, and spirit.

## Master Chakra Descriptions
## for Identification of Self and Others

*Reds* are natural leaders who know where people should be going and what they should be doing at any given time. They are always one step ahead of everyone else in terms of seeing the big picture and knowing what needs to be done to get there. They stay in the moment. They move quickly in an emergency to make sure everyone is okay and prevent problems before they happen by sticking close to the ground in a general way, through their teachings and their love. They love to stay in action in the physical world and work toward goals—getting everyone moving toward the goal—for the betterment of a group, not just themselves. They give you direction and purpose where it is lacking.

*Oranges* don't recognize rules or allow limitations to keep them from joy. They don't like hearing no and work on seeing your light and happiness so you can say yes to them if they need you to help them out. They want to be the life of the party. They bring you joy and happiness in spite of yourself. They connect you with what works in the sales-world. They shine their golden love on all so that no one can dislike them, and they bring others into the fold by including them in their stories and family of kooks. They take from the light, give to the light, and keep the divine purpose moving mostly in a direction toward joy and loving understanding when they are at their best. They give you counsel when everything seems under the weather.

*Yellows* disregard all mental activity if it does not lead to the higher mind and their one, singular goal. They reach for the highest ideal and the greatest goals; they can invent any structure, sacred joy, or means to get there if given time. They can build a time machine. They can reach their dreams. They find better ways to get from points A to Z because they care. To have their way accomplished—they find the maps, make them, or synthesize from yours. They are always looking for the best maps. Yellows look for the solution to counsel all others toward a better reality so that they too can experience the living truth of wisdom incarnate. They seek truth, find it, and help us all get outside the box through that. They love to share new solutions to old problems.

*Greens* never stop striving to find the solutions to problems, because systems that don't work are challenges, and they set up systems to help people succeed. They love to find balance, impart it to others, and mend, fix, or make whole that which doesn't seem to be working. They would just like things to work because it makes life better and it makes them feel calm. They have the capacity to remain tranquil, alone and separate, during hard times. They are the only color to do this well. They are the natural doctors, mechanics, and accountants of the world, doing their work out of compassion and love for spirit. They begin and end with the infinity sign, which is not only a sign of abundance, but of balance and health in its highest form.

*Blues* are not just teachers; they are masters of the art of teaching. It's the cause of knowledge and that it can transform lives that keeps them moving. They draw knowledge out of you and help you understand what you need to know next on your path. It is likely that when a blue talks, he or she will simultaneously teach for the enlightenment of the student. This is not the goal of others unless they are trying to get a point across. It is the blue master chakra default. The aim of the one who wishes to balance what *is* with what *isn't* is given to them so everyone may see they hold both opposites in their hands. Blues are passionate about equality, being fair and just, and uniting opposite forces for the greater good through the art of their teaching.

*Purples* are, according to my teacher Joseph Crane, "masters of the song and dance." As such, they use the flow and movement of body, sound, and light to create performances so that people can grow in spirit, evolve, learn more about themselves and others, and just generally get along. They might recite a poem. They might dramatize their conversation. They might show you love by cooking you a meal. They might create a really cool tepee for you to sleep in. They might direct a play. All this is for you to be able to explore yourself and your relationships so that you come to a greater understanding of the divine. They seek to unite across boundaries, acknowledging none.

*Violets* let everyone else go first and are able to become any of the other master chakras in order to help them do their jobs. They perform service-acts to help the world get back to normalcy. They will do anything it takes to assist the world in this process. Violets have an especially keen sense of understanding of how things work together and what is needed to uplift and heal the world and its people. They receive not only global visions, but very individualized approaches to helping people, which places them in the demand, and admiration, of all. They are kind in their approach and wish to offend no one. They come from a place of service and hope.

# 1

# MASTER
# CHAKRA QUIZ

Find out where your true gifts lie—which chakra is dominant in you. In each of the following sections of questions, please pick the description that describes you best. The quiz can be used to see which color(s) you might be and also as a learning tool to identify key characteristics of all the colors. TEST your mastery. If being used to identify your color, mark the number that best describes you under each section. If being used to test yourself on what you have learned, identify which color is being spoken of in each sentence.

### When you walk into a room

1. _____ You find a way to take charge of it.

2. _____ You share with others how you feel we can best function with whatever purpose has been established for everyone in this room—you question that purpose, though. Why are we here?

3. _____ You speak to others and enlighten them.

4. _____ You spend all your time making sure no one is hungry, sad, or lost. You comfort those who need it.

5. _____ You find a way to make people smile. Laughter follows in your wake.

6. _____ You see what needs to be fixed or straightened in this room. You search for the tools that are at hand, and, seeing that no one else cares, you get things working again.

7. _____ You're drawn to create a sculpture about what's going on in the room. You find the people interesting.

### At a concert, this sounds like you

1. _____ You don't care as much about this concert as you do about the new thing you're studying on your iPhone. If this new information turns out to be more engaging than the music, you'll read it instead.

2. _____ You sit in the back so you can watch everyone. If a fire starts in this place, you will lead everyone to safety. Going to the bathroom at intermission, you see two little girls playing in the water fountain and get them to stop.

3. _____ Immaculate in your appearance, you arrive at the concert looking flawless. You may or may not be the most fashionable person here, but no one matches your attention to detail. Now, you think you hear those speakers crackling...

4. _____ You go to the front of the pit and dance like there is no tomorrow, getting everyone around you to dance with you. After this, you and your new friends will go to three more parties, getting stuck at none for long.

5. _____ After making sure the kids of the family sitting next to you have water bottles (they were thirsty), you'll go back to the car and get blankets for your kids, since they're cold. Next, you relax into the supreme sense of the okayness of it all.

6. _____ You fall deeply into the music. You don't like it that people are looking at their iPhones. You put your arm around your sweetheart, pay attention to the ambience, all the sound qualities, and even the sunset.

7. _____You do not want to listen to this concert because you'd rather talk to your neighbor. You can't stop talking because there are so many people here and you have so much to say.

### Choose how you react when you're having a really bad day

1. _____You think you're not good enough. Because of this, everything sucks.

2. _____You use people to get what you want.

3. _____You're angry—and resentful. People don't get how their actions have consequences.

4. _____While normally you take responsibility, today you'd rather do nothing.

5. _____You're self-centered; no one is good enough for you.

6. _____You blame other people—everything is their fault.

7. _____You disconnect from people around you and hole up in your room.

### You are passionate about...

1. _____Finding something fun to do immediately or right before something gets boring. You can make anything fun, and...you will find a way.

2. _____Reading, writing, and gathering wisdom. Being a daily intellectual. Finding balance. Caring about people, social consciousness, the physical pastime of your choice... telling other people what you think they should know.

3. _____Being peace. Finding the best solution to a problem, then using it. Curing people. Releasing their pain. Fixing their broken stuff.

4. _____Putting the pieces together, and you can spend hours doing it. In fact, you spend more time doing your research than most. You're all about placing your goal ahead of you and striving to reach it.

5. _____Either expressing yourself through art or science. Life is about love, acting when the emotions are right, and beauty. Life is about making things. It's about being in relationship with others so the love shines through.

6. _____Having a lot of courage and faith. After all, it's relatively easy for you to believe in the unseen and see it happening even before there is any evidence that it will. You're powerful in your beliefs about the future.

7. _____Doing any of the things you just read about so that you can help people.

**In the presence of others, you're good at ...**

1. _____Showing someone what went wrong and showing them how to make it right.

2. _____Identifying other people's emotions when even they didn't realize what feelings were deep down about that stuff they experienced.

3. _____Giving other people advice. They even ask for it.

4. _____Putting another person first and clearing your schedule to help them.

5. _____Telling the truth.

6. _____Bringing the light back into someone's eyes after telling them something they needed to know. They will never be the same.

7. _____Making someone smile when they were down.

See the final page of this chapter for your answers!

## Master Chakra Traps

The traps of each master chakra describe ways in which you tend to be out of alignment with your gifted self. Identifying which key traps seem to fit you best overall is another step in the process of seeing which soul-ray you were born on. You may not resonate with each trap listed—it's more about identifying the whole picture, and there are even more traps than discussed here.

For more information about how to emerge from these traps and their brethren, see your master chakra workbook.

*Reds* in their traps are larger than life, just like in their gifts, but they can be an angry, forceful beast. Focused on themselves, egotistical—blaming everyone else instead of taking responsibility—they could be loud or quiet about it. They can blame you for what they didn't do. They can blame you for all the things they see you didn't do (which might be true, but still—they don't have to rule you). They can intimidate with their anger, and then again, they could just try to control you and organize against you. They'll be stubborn and refuse to listen to you. They have to have their way at all costs, and they could use you for their purposes instead of respecting what you want. Or they'll just sit there and do absolutely nothing, giving away their power—either to you or someone else. If you say something to them about how they are, or even insult them, they'll genuinely believe you. You could say anything to them. They'd believe it whether it was true or not. It's a big downfall.

*Oranges* in their traps don't have an ability to stop moving to the next thing. On and on and on, they never stop moving, and because of that, when they can't achieve something great, they're stuck, if they didn't stick with anything long enough. Or they have to run from trouble, creating situations where people turn against them because they've broken so many rules and didn't have proper boundaries. Oranges in their traps can lie outright and refuse to take responsibility for what they did. They can get too wrapped up in their feelings and create any story to get them out. They can over-analyze their feelings, which takes them away from both joy and reality. Then, when they realize they've done something wrong, they punish themselves. They can't get out of being negative. They might get addicted to having fun in the wrong ways and that will sabotage their ability to be healthy.

*Yellows* in their traps disregard their feelings and can use their ego to get what it wants by being able to disregard yours. Anything is possible when you have no feelings and don't care about the other person's. The sky's the limit because any behavior would then be possible, since everyone and everything is then able to be objectified. Yellows could isolate themselves from the community and all individuals at large by simply never leaving their home. Yellows don't need to be social in their traps. They don't believe anything that can't be verified scientifically or logically, and they forget Spirit. They won't acknowledge the truth inherent in the unseen and are too stuck on facts. They can always be controlling and demand you follow their paths of truth without letting you figure things out for yourself. Then again, they might just be scattered in their mind and make no sense—even hoping you'll follow them, even when they don't live in reality and can't come to conclusions about the truth often enough.

*Greens* in their traps focus too much on the process, which is always going to be their first love, but still—when they walk too far away from the human element involved, they can treat people like objects. They only care about what they're doing with them and forget to care about the person him or herself. Greens become unorganized in their traps. They don't clean their house and they don't fix their own problems—they neglect themselves. They don't get themselves out of their own traps; they just keep focusing on other people. Greens can be annoying to some people because they won't stop finding things about others to critique. They see too many things that need to be fixed and then try to fix what doesn't need fixing, sometimes breaking something so that eventually they will be able to fix it again. They stop doing things for the sake of God and do them for themselves instead when they become power hungry. When they stop starting with spirit, they start doing things from ego that might hurt others, including manipulating their money with schemes, instead of helping them balance themselves and follow their heart with finances.

*Blues* in their traps might think you are stupid because you can't understand things the way they do. They can think they are above others because of their knowledge. They can even be like this with other blues. They sometimes forget to be emotional, forget about how to come from love when teaching wisdom. They might lose their emotional, mental, physical, or spiritual balance, and whenever this happens, they can't teach others as effectively, if at all. Sometimes blues just stop teaching because they don't want to. Being quiet when there is clearly something they feel called to say—not taking that risk to speak, is a trap just as much as talking too much and not letting others have their wisdom and their say. They can get angry, resentful, and bitter when they think about the past, about man's inhumanity to man, about anything that isn't working well. They lose control of their mind. They can be dramatic, thinking everything that happens is either the best or the worst of what is. Creating drama is a classic blue trap—dramas usually begin with the way we communicate. A final blue trap is leaving people behind too often—mostly because they can't humble themselves to communicate and solve the issue. This is a consequence of holding yourself separate from others, which they come by naturally.

*Purples* in their traps focus on gaining material compensation for their work to the point where it affects the work and degrades it. This can happen in any number of ways: either they stop creating great stuff because they're so focused on marketing it, or they figure out from having been able to command big ticket prices in the past that they can pass off lesser creations as better. They sell out, or sell the art of creation, creation itself, which leaves them in poverty in the mind and heart. They create unhelpful art, that which people don't like to see. Or, they dislike having to wear what's already in their closet, use the art supplies they already own, or forgo buying a new shirt over buying food they need to eat; they won't make do and demand luxury when it isn't a good idea to have it. Even the people aren't good enough for them when they take on the privileged mindset. They can trigger people too much and destroy what they don't love—destroy a relationship because there is something they don't like about it. They refuse to take people out of turmoil. They spend too much time focused on themselves and not enough on bringing love into the world, however that might be possible at the time.

*Violets* have a penchant for sacrificing themselves in their traps. They think it's what they need to do: not take care of themselves and only take care of someone else, but then they blame that person for their own missing pieces, pieces that went missing while they were too busy to help themselves. Violets get walked on by others when they don't set boundaries and empower themselves to choose who to help and who to ignore—and how much to do for the people they are helping. Violets lose when they don't delegate; they think they have to do it all. It's a state of martyr complex. They also claim moral authority in their traps (because of the martyr complex) where they manipulate others into doing their bidding. They might be able to get things done because they are nice, but are those things always in the best interests of everyone around? They can refuse to tell people the truth in fear it might hurt them, making situations better for the short term, but not for the long term. The people around them, then, believe things about themselves that aren't true—even believing the violet likes them when they do not. Violets stop speaking up, stop taking action to help things happen in a good way, and fake their goodness—doing things just to get rewarded in the world, the land of dust, instead of because they love their divine connection and want to further it by making the world into Eden again.

## Quiz Answers

*Question 1: When You Walk Into a Room:* 1, Red. 2, Yellow. 3, Blue. 4, Violet. 5, Orange. 6, Green. 7, Purple.

*Question 2: At a Concert:* 1, Yellow. 2, Red. 3, Green. 4, Orange. 5, Violet. 6, Purple. 7, Blue.

*Question 3: How You React When You're Having a Really Bad Day:* 1, Violet. 2, Green. 3, Blue. 4, Red. 5, Purple. 6, Orange. 7, Yellow.

*Question 4: You are Passionate About:* 1, Orange. 2, Blue. 3, Green. 4, Yellow. 5, Purple. 6, Red. 7, Violet.

*Question 5: In the Presence of Others:* 1, Green. 2, Purple. 3, Red. 4, Violet. 5, Yellow. 6, Blue. 7, Orange.

# 2

# REDS: THE NATURAL LEADERS

When your spiritual gift is located in a chakra, you see its possibilities and issues everywhere around you: in people, places, and things. You cannot separate your lens, or focus, from the object you are focusing on. Reds do share their expertise with you, and in this way let you borrow their red-colored glasses. They, having been bent by a certain light, will bend light for you. You do not need to do it for yourself. This is their job.

## A Basic Definition

Reds, with the spiritual gift formed by the root chakra, easily draw, through their connection with God, visions on how to move forward in life. They tend to act as though the wind is always at their back, and they stay attitudinally in action at all times, especially when they take action and give orders. They strike out into new territory to structure light into the world.

As a boss, they move people into action to fulfill a purpose either they or someone else has decided. They will get you started in a direction you aren't accustomed to. And they personally set their sights on visions of how to be better—for themselves and for you. Faith, or hope in the certainty of something, is a state of being that allows reds to openly create their reality with confidence. And, since they like to focus on success so much and involve us in their plans whenever possible, they get the operation off the ground and turn it into a moving train. This is what makes them worthy of the title of "leader."

## Red Gifts

Reds are overarching, big-picture people. They prefer to spend time telling others what to do and watching over them than spending their days taking care of minutiae. It makes them good at running businesses. It also makes them good at helping someone believe in themselves. Because their gift is focused in the physical realm, they concentrate on the bottom line. They always keep the achievement of their objectives in front of themselves. They want to engage you in the objectives that they come up with and encourage you to develop yourself so you can accomplish what you desire. Sometimes reds prefer to give orders directly, and at other times they enjoy leading from behind, inspiring you to be courageous and explaining what you need to do to get the results you want. Here are both strategies.

## Leading Out Front

Reds might approach people assembled by getting their attention and giving a short speech that consists of an overview of what must be done. Or, then again, a short sentence may be enough, depending on the context. Their reference points are often physical. For example, when leading a workshop of over a hundred people, a red I know once got up on stage, told us what the purpose of the workshop was in terms of what change we were going to create in humanity, told us about a couple of the ways we were going to do that, let us know where the bathrooms were, and then gave the floor to someone else. "Explanation" was left to others. It also happened with a red boss of mine. I marveled at how little time was really spent getting up and talking, because the talking he did was always about where we were going and what we needed to do. How we were going to get there and the reasoning and logic of it were just not available from this person, someone I respected. But they don't want to give the rest, because the rest is up to us!

But what if a red manages an entire organization on an ongoing basis? What will she say in a staff meeting? She will review the goals that have been achieved. She will acknowledge people who did well. She will state where the group is going next. During group discussions of obstacles, or during times in the meeting when other staff members are traditionally supposed to inform others of something, she will keep a keen eye on whether or not what is said is germane to what her goals are. Reds realize that some people need more of an explanation than others. She may let you explain the rationale or process to others, or she might tell you to do it later in a different setting. Reds don't like people to linger too long in thoughts, feelings, explanations, or stories. This can sometimes impede them from even getting the information they need to lead. Still—they will do it to keep everyone on (their) track. Heaps of details and digressions can be more difficult to get through to them depending on their density and relative relationship to the big picture; if you can't get to the point and relate it to their goal, you will be eaten like a wounded fish in shark-infested waters.

And the least favorite item of all, for a boss, the de facto role of every red, even those low in a hierarchy? Excuses. Reds prefer reasons. A reason is a material, responsible explanation that proves you did do work, you just didn't finish it yet because there was a snowstorm (physical obstruction) and you couldn't drive your car to the gas station. An excuse is an explanation that communicates you did not focus yourself toward your goal and allowed another concern to get in your way. In other words, you did not apply sufficient effort to affect a material change in your work. Your results are the criteria that reveal whether or not you have an excuse or a reason. Rather than dwelling on excuses, reds will express straightforward dismissal of them. Complaining doesn't feel grounding to a red. Neither do flimsy arguments, such as those based on tradition for tradition's sake, appearances, the misapplication of facts, or the scrambling of details in order to obfuscate. These techniques, when used, will often lead to a serious questioning of that person's intelligence and motives. At bottom, the red simply cannot understand why a person would want to stand in the way of progress. They can feel it when someone's actions and intentions will lead to an actual creation. You cannot hide where you are on your path. A red in his or her giftedness will focus on helping those who are off task in whatever they are doing and aren't truly producing results. If necessary, a red can get them some help so they can proceed, if encouragement or tough love isn't enough to refocus the person on the goal.

As they move their organization forward, a red will work to keep everyone in their group on the path through thematic comments about what is being done or how it needs to change. Reds say what they mean and mean what they say. They will stick by their word. They will be the force that holds the line on what is aimed for. They do make it clear what they expect from others they lead and how they expect it to be done. Yet when they discuss how they want something done, their words will be brief. Otherwise they risk confusing those that look to them for help and losing their attention. They risk making them think they aren't responsible for coming up with their own actions. They judge by the physical, which means they look to the physical world to see where things can be improved.

It is up to you and your associates to figure out how to carry out what the red wants you to do in an ongoing, developed way—the structure, the nitty-gritty, the knowledge needed. You get to do all the work behind the process, or the philosophy, they suggest. That's your work. Reds don't want to get involved in it, layer upon layer; they like to stay in the top layer much of the time, though they will pitch in and mulch it. You will notice that when they are in a student role and learning from you, they do want what you want—more guidance, not less. But in their role as leaders they don't overly teach, they lead. They will teach you what you need to know to get what they are saying. They don't teach to teach. So, in general, reds stick with giving top-down instructions and making big-picture comments—often from a smiling, happy, confident place, or one that is in solidarity either with you or the group. They don't alienate when they don't explain. When leading out-front, they do mean business.

### Leading from Behind

Leading from behind describes a feminine style of leadership reds use to continue to lead from a point where they feel everyone knows what they are doing and what is at stake. This becomes all about building people up, going behind the scenes, encouraging someone, fixing things that go wrong—with or without assistance—making follow-up decisions, and bringing people to consensus. Once the goal has been set and people begin working, it is necessary to coordinate all aspects of the team. They want other people to take their roles and do their part. They like to see that unfold before their eyes. The cheerleader in them will come out and tell everyone what a great job they are doing and remind them of all of their good qualities. When someone falls down a hole, the red will dig them out of it and get them moving again. This could be a literal or a metaphorical hole. Reds have your back. As a child I was once close to used to say about her red mother, "mommas coming to get you out."

Reading people and seeing their strengths is really necessary for a red, because non-reds can forget their own capabilities and fail to work up to their potential. A red likes to activate this potential by using a positive attitude that brings love to their employees or followers while giving them some tips on what to do once they are in progress. Reds respect that people go through a long process to get something done. In their gifts, they allow these processes to occur and manage by checking in and looking at each person. Reds are drawn to the places where they are needed at just the right times. This is the essence of leading from behind—it's not an egomaniacal approach that demands someone do something now (where you might have a red do this in their traps). It's an approach that is highly intuitive and contextual, even motherly.

When giving the proper pressure necessary—the push, which others need to go forth and do what they need to do to help us all succeed—reds inspire. So, they will make you think you can do anything they know you are capable of at the core of your being. Reds are people who give you confidence in yourself. It's a given with them that you to live up to it, to the potential that they know and see in you. This is why hanging around a red can make a person's self-doubt melt away and increase their innate sense of confidence and know-how. It can be very reassuring to be around someone who knows where you are supposed to go and what you are supposed to do and expects you to be fully capable of that. They don't care about what you think you cannot do, but rather what they think you can. And they may not even be aware that there is a disconnect going on, that you are in doubt, because they can't afford doubt. So they just present to you the future as they see it, without your doubts.

Reds find the road you can walk on so you can grow and prosper. They give you a mission and help you develop it through their management style. Red thinking automatically organizes itself according to this intention. This goal puts them ahead of others, and its weighty significance is what lets them beat competition and create strategy that succeeds. Reds will always be first and they will always be last. They head up projects, and they also sometimes move in only once those projects are finished. They wait for completion, then start to lead. They will always be the bookends. They never stop striving to reach a goal—they expand it into the next biggest goal that they can possibly reach. They are the leaders, and they hold you in gratitude because of that. Without you, they would be nothing.

### Protection

Like any mother, reds protect their children. It's one of the reasons they winnow down the group of possible actions to the most essential. This does not just happen in work contexts; it can happen when a group of friends goes to the mall. The red will tend to keep tabs on the group. Because staying in the moment is essential for them, and things can only get done in the present, they are able to serve as an ever-watchful sentry. So even if it's a minor chiefdom, such as managing a shopping group, reds will take it on. Non-reds can get distracted and let people wander around for too long. Remember, reds never forget that it is non-reds that they manage, in addition to the few reds that might be below them in a management chain. Non-reds understand that a side road can take us places we want to go, places important to us. Reds, however, have less use for getting distracted. They know that what you do the most is what you'll get done.

Sometimes what other colors do gets them in trouble because they tend not to take getting in trouble as seriously as reds. This is because potential danger often doesn't seem so dangerous to a non-red. They self-sabotage too easily, according to a red. This principle refers to the actions that we take that put us little by little in a state of distress. We are usually not aware of these actions, or their consequences, while we are performing them.

For example, a red will see it if someone experiences financial hardship and wants to help that person take control. They will suggest actions that get that person out of harm's way, such as changing their view of debt and releasing its importance—its role in a human's suffering. They would then suggest the person struggling get a better or different job. A red will offer the support needed—starting with the mental conditioning and the emotional release from the strictures of others, ending with the spiritual grounding and the physical support—to get that person to safer ground. A red's direction is clear and distinct. They make it easier for you to follow their directions because they get to the point, have courage, and give you courage. When you are able to go to them for continued input, you will start to turn your situation around. That's because they focus on the bottom line and put you in the driver's seat at the same time.

We don't notice our struggle until it gets severe because we've become so comfortable with the discomfort. Reds see what's going on and how the path has gotten bent. They create a strategy for liberation. In the above example, it was faster to help the person change their beliefs about finances than suggest they explore finding a different career right away. That was suggested at a later date after careful consideration. Reds base their strategy on the battle that rages in the person. They choose to first stop the bleeding. Later they will set the bone. Triage is necessary, but all of the strategies they apply will keep the person on the path, which is the same as keeping them safe and moving forward, overall.

Reds constantly delineate for themselves (and you) what is and is not a distraction, what is and is not harmful. If you think about it, someone has to be that point person, that person that keeps everyone on track, working together for a good cause in the most linear way possible. That is what it's all about for the leader. Isn't it nice to know that someone is paying attention 24-7, just because they are being themselves? And isn't it nice to know that a red has been doing it since day one?

*From Crown to Toe, a Leader*

If a question is asked, then starting from the crown chakra, they receive their answers. Their intuition comes from divine inspiration. They get their extremely far-ahead and pin-pointed intuition by being enlightened with knowledge from above in such a way as it comes into their crown chakra and into every cell of their body. They just get, all at once, a great big concept that an individual needs to move forward on.

So, they physically feel their spiritual visions, which is where their big picture stems from. Reds are close to the earth and their energy always focuses in a downward motion, bringing other people's concerns, ideas, and energy down to the ground, where they will shake out as real or not. Their answers to your questions often have a physical cast, using sensory images, and their tone of voice reflects their connection with action repeated on the earth plane. They care about causes and what caused something to happen—the beginning, the start. Then, things must keep clicking into a physical reality for forward motion to occur. All things from above extend into the bottom of the system—the root of the tree for a red. They love to compare an idea to a physical reality.

*A Reason to Lead*

They are most gratified when the group they are helping reaches its object. If reds do not lead a formal group, they can still have a group of people, consisting of whomever it is they usually socialize with. When the group is the reason and inspiration for their vision, it's easy for them to stay in their light, tell people what to do, and be well received when doing so. So, the group is the red's leader. They believe that they exist to help the group, that the group nominated them, and it becomes their reason for living. They experience courage within themselves at the lip of danger, because they can subordinate all personal, lesser concerns to their overarching vision for the group, and give it their loyalty. A great example of how this occurs can be found in the television series, *Vikings*. The leader, Ragnar Lothbrok, only wants to fight foreigners and take their land in order to give it to his own young people to farm. His people didn't have enough land, they were in a crisis, so he rose to power as a red to help his community. His passion is children, both his own children and the next generation of his people. This textbook example of a red shows how concerned reds ultimately are with the future of physical survival. They will lay down their life for the group and the people they love. While doing it, they will move as steadily as possible toward their goals in as linear a way as possible, reluctant to waste time.

### Good with Emergencies

Reds' standards for safety and survival are high. So are our root chakras. They don't just give orders in a boardroom or family meeting; they can give you orders in the darkest of situations. In the book *Dear America: Letters Home from Vietnam*, a soldier writes that he survived the war by finding a man who knew where to go and what to do to survive, by never letting him out of his sight. That person showed internal calm in the face of war. Natural leaders can do this because not only do they react instinctually to life, but because they are so intimately bound to group survival, progress, and development. They will keep their life as long as they can, and go back to God when necessary to save others.

One all-around example of a red is a high school history teacher I knew, who was getting his PhD in history—the history of war, while teaching. This was a teacher who led, first and foremost. He was famous for his ability to say anything he pleased in the classroom. He did it using his intuition and his direct attitude. Still, he often made jokes and laughed with his students. Seating students in the room according to political affiliation, he gave everyone nicknames that related to who they were. This was meant to either challenge them to be better or acknowledge their importance. He would tell his students what they thought, then ask them what they thought. The point was to help them connect their thoughts to political dynamics so they could see their place in the world. In the age before the internet, he imparted to his students an internet of empowerment principles based on the study of victories and failures in war and of groups of people throughout history. He gave his students college-level reading and assigned long papers for them to write, many of which he did not read. He was preparing them for college, life—like it was a battle that could be won.

## Setting Boundaries

Reds direct the traffic both physically and in the sense of who should do what. That's how they can be equally responsive to the high school class, the crisis in your life, and the corporate world. They confront so many different situations, but they do so from the same viewpoint: as a challenge to be met instead of a problem to be solved. Setting boundaries is a requisite task for reds, who clearly perceive differences between what is yours, mine, and someone else's. This goes not only for possessions, but life purposes, behavior, advice—you name it. If someone is behaving in a way that impinges on someone else's ability to decide for themselves, reds will see it. You being sovereign of yourself serves them being sovereign of you. You can't be as good of a worker if you can't stay strong. They want to empower you because they know you accomplish more when you are more. They aim high when they see what is possible for you; they let you know what you need in your life to be able to move forward, so that we can all move forward together. In their gifts, they want you to be able to work independently.

## Commitment to Clearing Obstacles, Reaching Goals

Functional reds find ways around obstacles. They're always practicing staying in action by default of being always in action, so obstacles are immediately dealt with rather than tabled. They have a habit of off-handedly dealing with them in a way where others know they cannot obstruct. One of their top values is following through, because actions can't be compounded to build something when commitment by those vested are missing, and reds want to be the example. They are able to commit to actions, and they value the same trait in others. Commitment ensures a seamless flow from goal to end result.

## Red Traps

### *Lack of Leadership*

Deciding that they are not the leaders, and refusing to lead, keeps reds stuck and creates dissatisfaction. Trouble can come in many forms, including a group without a leader that is plagued by aimlessness. Reds can play victims, blame, and whine—not to mention sit on the couch and do nothing. In the shadows, their ego looks to take them down by letting them off the hook. They checkout or run away in their traps. They stop being brave.

### *Starting a Fight Without Fear of Repercussion*

There is usually a gray area between gifts and traps. When a red will push a person around in order to test their own strength, it can be acceptable if that person is strong enough to take them. If not, like all unwanted gifts, this can be seen as tough love that knows no bounds and, in the worst cases, bullying. When people are not ready to fight you, and don't rise to the occasion, your motive may not appear to be in your favor. Reds then cross boundaries instead of set them.

### Not Exhibiting Understanding, Blaming, and Ruling

Let's say someone isn't contributing to the bottom line, and the red is in her traps. She will simply fire the person, giving up on them, perhaps with obvious discontent. Treating a non-emergency like an emergency is a recipe for fear, and ruling by fear is the familiar territory of the ego out of control. Getting very egotistically angry and out of control is a red trap. Blaming the employees instead of taking responsibility for what happened is a key red trap.

When a red asks you to do something their way, it's because it's from their philosophy. But it doesn't have to be self-serving, and when it is, then such a goal is not created for the sake of everyone but rather for the individual satisfaction of that red, and that is exactly what has made people hate leaders. Leaders need to be influenced by those around them to the point where the leader is stitching together a patchwork quilt of everyone else and being the person that guides the entire quilt through the sewing machine. You have to start with the people and make sure they need what's being given. Dysfunctional reds feel like dictators because they do not understand how to best give people what they need. They are not taking a high enough perspective. Their intuition or connection with God is not being attended to.

### Disagreeing with Reality: Believing Lies

It's ironic that a red would sometimes put up a wall so as not to hear good sense but bring down their personal wall just to believe someone's lie about them. Believing other people's lies instead of sticking to their own self-direction and knowing their own goodness is a major trap for the red spiritual gift. This is how they allow the people they are supposed to lead to take them down. When other people try to tell a red something not true about themselves, or blame them for something they didn't do or something that isn't true, they succeed if the red believes it. Reds can let themselves be self-critical and seek the input of others, but still trust themselves. If they don't, their choices degenerate into a series of uncertainties that reflect the lie, or the false motive that someone placed on them. Ultimately, the red becomes bandied about by other people's lies to the point where they don't know themselves or can't focus on who they are. People can react to power by undermining the person who holds it because they are jealous, incompetent, or worse. Sometimes a red will have to realize that when a person isn't ready for their leadership, they might need to ignore it or overtly resist it. Not everyone wants to follow the leader. Sometimes a red will have to realize that a person isn't ready for their leadership—which starts with encouragement, and even compliments, as I have seen many a red open with. Each red will have developed at least some of their own strategies for healthy leadership. It all depends on how much time that person has spent living in their giftedness to do so, versus their traps.

*In Summation*

It's a red's job not only to lead out front but also from behind; to believe in you when you cannot believe in yourself. The red master chakra gift trusts that it knows what you need to do to succeed, and shares it. This gift is feminine—it carries you by inspiring you to put your best foot forward, without doubts or fears, and stay in the moment. Reds show you where to go while encouraging you along the way, helping you with boundaries, guiding you to justice and staying present, holding you accountable when necessary, and loving it when you succeed.

## Famous People with a Red Master Chakra

People with the red master chakra have the potential to be some of the most powerful people guiding us toward the future. Some famous examples of reds include George Washington, who was a general and the first president, and Oprah, who wants to take everyone to the light and holds people accountable on her show. Take a moment to think about someone in your life who might be a red.

# 3

# Oranges: The Natural Promoters

Today we shut down much of what gives people joy, like going against the grain, following your heart instead of your head, making money—and the list goes on. The fact is, anything that creates joy causes us to evolve. Still, we have cut off so many sources of it, including simple pleasures and the right to be carefree, that it's one of the most sought-after states of being. The secret is, everyone has different angles on happiness, and when we share them, we expand our awareness and become more appealing. The spirit of the orange chakra helps us re-define joy and remember any route to it so we become perfect, whole, and complete in our selves.

## A Basic Definition

Oranges are blessed with being good at sexuality, play, relation-ships, and letting things go. Many of us have a hard time get-ting our sacral chakra moving, but oranges in their giftedness do not; they respect, understand, and model how to handle these topics. It's related to their highest expression of gifted-ness in promoting: lifting things to a higher level. With their certain intuition, they see how you can move forward and what you are willing to do, before you do. The natural promoters, in sales and outside the field, work hard to gain the happiness of others so that they themselves can feel divine love. People who create experiences, find circumstances, and see oppor-tunities for others to have fun have an abundance of positive energy that attracts others. Their talents aim to promote you to a higher level of vibration, and joy is the highest emotional vibration there is. They do not always succeed in helping the rest of the colors remain happy, because sometimes we do not like what an orange must do to get us there, or what we need to do to stay there, but most non-oranges have a hard time with sacral chakra tasks, and oranges can make the difference, and often do, in helping us release the constraints and integrate joy even when we're on the opposing track.

They really love being motivational speakers, even experts in appreciation. Oranges want to encourage you to enjoy your life and be the best you can be. They can't help but see the promotable qualities in you. They are frank when they speak of you admiringly, but also impermeable to contradiction.

Because they only hear, see, and say "yes," it's easy for you to be convinced by their manner that they mean what they say about you—about anything. There is an internal acceptance and motivation moving through them that allows you to soak in and believe their opinions—their certainties. People are their focus, giving them center stage. They show you who you are and what you could be, in joy. Wouldn't it be great, they say, if you had your own business and got to the head of your class because you're so smart and creative? After they've pumped you up, they might also offer the best humanity has to offer: a good car, a connection at work, an educational program, and more. They may or may not make counteroffers.

## Orange Gifts

### Having Fun

Oranges shine when they are having fun, which they do without a second thought; they can be like live wires. Even oranges who appear calm vibrate with joyful energy that picks you up. They may ask you questions or tell you things that constantly focus you on what is coming up ahead that is a joyful opportunity for you. Who could argue with that? If you want to find an orange, look for the twinkle in their eye. An orange who is suppressed in their gifts will not come across as happy, but will exhibit a high amount of nervous energy. It takes quite a bit of conditioning to suppress this energy, so you will still see it as moving under their surface even when they are sad. Their energy sparkles, crackles, and shines.

*The Case of the Lollipop Loophole*
One day in Østerås, Norway, while on vacation, I spontaneously decided to stop in a grocery store on my way home. The grocery store just seemed to call me. After filling my arms with more than I expected (because it just felt so fun to get the vegetables specifically packaged for fall, and I wanted to have snacks for my movie—something I normally would not buy in the United States), I got in line at the checkout. Orange energy had already been dominating my entire experience so far. The checkout guy immediately said hi and began ringing up my items. When I paid with a credit card, he didn't miss a beat. I was very surprised by that—I had already baffled numbers of cashiers who were not used to people without PIN numbers for credit cards. Not this one. He simply turned around, picked up a lollipop, gave it to me, and said, "Please sign here." I took the lollipop with hesitation. I said, "really?" He said, "Yes, I promise." He said it with such authority and conviction and purr of reassurance there was no way I could argue.

After I signed, I said, "You've never done that before, have you!?" At that point, knowing I was not from Norway, he said, "Have a good night," though loudly, as I was already walking out of the store. He was smiling when I turned around.

*The Case of the Taxation Loophole*
One day I was getting ready to redo my taxes from a prior year, so I picked up the phone and called a referral I had on hand for this purpose. The tax preparer claimed he had never lost an

audit. He insisted I see him in person. He looked through all of my information and determined that my business taxes had been submitted under the wrong designation; my company was a corporation, not a sole-proprietary. He then found $1200 that was owed to me based on this false designation. Many of my expenses previously reported had been claimed conservatively. All of a sudden I questioned why I was sitting in my chair in front of him. Why could we not have had this conversation over the phone? When I asked him why I couldn't call him he stated his phone was bugged ... he told me he was concerned about getting phone calls because he knew things that the IRS did not, that they were watching him. He pointed to a large 1920s-looking book he had stayed up all night reading. (Oranges get so excited about the things they decide to learn about that they can't sleep.) I Ie questioned several of my recent, though minor, tax payment decisions, leaving me with the impression that I had unwittingly "donated" money to the IRS. Finally, he told me it was up to me to use the designation I had chosen, or not. No one could decide but me ... I could be free to stand outside whatever I had put on paper. (This is typical of oranges who do not recognize the living reality of rules.) He conveyed to me how to not feel constrained by IRS oversight.

### The Case of the Constant Course-Corrector

I once had a boyfriend nicknamed "Tumbleweed." The Tumbleweed loved to have possessions and jobs when it suited him, and not when it didn't. There was a method to his madness. In the course of less than a year, he moved from an 80K job as a nurse, because he suspected he might get in trouble, to working for himself as a stockbroker, two hundred miles from where he previously lived. He made a thousand dollars right before my eyes on the day he decided to do it. However, that was the first and last time he made this money. Since it was too much fun working for himself, he kept doing it, not caring if he didn't get good results. So, he moved to a cabin in the woods in northern Minnesota, which was really a trailer, since he wasn't making great trades. When that was no longer juicy, he sold his Winnebago and talked about getting a job in Arizona for months before finally getting one—in the back of the woods. After a few months, Arizona looked better, so he went there to be a nurse once more. He had landed in a warmer place with better people who appreciated him. Money was not important, it was a means to obtain the fun that he deserved. (This is a common orange view of money.) The Tumbleweed was an expert at following his highest excitement.

Judging by his nickname, he had done this before...An orange in his gifts follows his bliss and will for the greater good of all. Usually, if any action results in creating more love, then it's light-bearing. Tumbleweed's actions did create more joy in his life and showed a higher degree of self-love than many people would be willing to embrace. However, he also showed a lack of trust that other people could help him work through his issues and stay at jobs that may have only been temporarily unpleasant. They don't have to run away. Even so, the question of having gifts and traps is all the same to an orange in the middle. An orange in their traps refuses to make a commitment to a course of action, and an orange in their gifts follows their bliss and does not settle for less. Sometimes, only a jury can decide if an orange is on the side of light or not.

## Orange Influence

We all need to determine how to live in our gifts; it's an individual choice. So oranges can experiment with what makes them and others happy. Otherwise how will they know when too many boundaries have been crossed? Of course their openness to fun is already deeper and wider than anyone else's. Their boundaries are not the same as yours, and they don't always know where they stop. Those of us without orange as a spiritual gift make choices based on our own core motivations, and because of this, we might forgo integrating joy into our lives. We forget. But that's what they are always seeking.

That's why they are good at helping you to achieve something glorious, whether that be a fun afternoon, an entire career change, or more risk-taking. They get your sacral chakra in flow so you can create things in your life that you desire. They focus you on how to feel better so you'll make a great choice. They are the joy bringers. You know when a conversation needs to end. They know before you know. True happiness, for them, is found in not being bound, as in for "too long." Oranges will move on—as in move away—from the following: experiences, people, and situations that make them feel sad. They don't like to be around too much seriousness, sadness, and loneliness. When things are just okay, they find something to say and say it in the most hopeful way, even if it's just the latest news, to help you remember your joy. They can get a "been there, done that" feeling very easily. For what makes them happy is something new that makes them happy. They need lots of alone time because they love to get their energy back so they can go out of the house again. It's all about them—and you—because eventually they will turn their presence into a gift for you again. They love getting out after they're done being alone, and they relish dance. If you're sitting too long or doing one thing for a long time, you're not really dancing in a feminine flow from activity to activity. So … you're not having "fun." Oranges understand how to move. They are the lives of the party, naturally. No matter how good they get at living in their gifts, they may still need help staying on track with what they are doing currently. Focus is key, but not always easy to come by. An average orange can be interruptive, because there is a timing in all things—of this they see and perceive. They're looking for that shiny object. That does help them help you.

When you are not doing well, they will either try to joke you out of your mood, take you with them to have fun, or give you counsel. These three strategies, which I'll call "short, mid, and long term," allow them to keep us up and prevent us from dwelling on the down times. Let's take a look at these three approaches, because one of the biggest parts of being an orange for others is to bring us up.

### Short-Term Techniques for Masterful Self-Awareness

Their short-term strategy for making you happy is to make you laugh or feel good about yourself. To make you laugh, they'll find either a joke you find funny or an embarrassing question. If it takes a well-placed comment to do that, they will say it. Sometimes this is offensive, but it usually does achieve its objective: the changing of your perspective. If they have done that, if they have gotten your attention away from the sad thing and onto something that feels better, they have done their work. They have either made happiness come alive or gotten you closer to it, even if they had to go below the belt (around your defenses) to make it happen. Their next strategy, the mid-term one, is to involve you in something.

### Mid-term Strategies for Helping Keep You Up

They could involve you in anything—for example, going out to lunch, or taking a break to have a popcorn party. These are spur-of-the-moment things. They will host an impromptu get-together. They will buy you something (a lotto ticket just to see the look on your face if you win five bucks.) They will point out that someone thinks you are cute. They are always watching to see if they can find something with to the point of having fun, and will take you with them all the way to the end. They will stealthily and with much encouragement involve you in these things (new products, new friends, new adjustments) to see if they can achieve their objective of changing your frame of mind.

### Long-term Methods to Get You to Gold

Their long-term-strategy is more about giving you perspective on how your experiences contribute to an eventual happiness, helping you take stock of the now. They point out happiness in the moment that you just haven't seen yet, because you haven't yet learned what you should do about the situation. Their job is to get you out of it. If they can't directly jack you out of your old flowerpot, they will go over things that have happened so you can see what the moment holds for you. When they hold counsel like this, strategizing on how to get you off the ground, they help you see what the bright sides are in what you have gone through. In order for you to move forward and be successful, you must see how great things really are underneath. Oranges also need to take care of what has to happen in the people around you in order for you to be happy in a long-term way, so when they give input, they will talk about how other people contribute to the problem and what moves you could make, as if everyone is on a chess board. Going beyond counsel, they will put themselves out of their way for you. They will find ways to get you or themselves out of almost any hot water.

### The Case of the Reliably Loyal Alibi

One orange I know was able to save an employee from job loss over a long period of time. This orange was a good advocate, having honed her skills in high school through such escapades as hiding her trips to Florida with her boyfriend from her parents, and at the same time talking her teachers into giving her good grades during that time so she didn't have to do any home-work while she was gone. She had witnessed the new employee's predecessor get fired (a thing no orange wants to see) and was determined not to let it happen again. She had a gift at the sacral chakra, the gift of the feminine: the gift of motherhood.

When the new employee was being targeted by the old supervisor, our orange friend would simply walk into the boss's office and start talking about the new employee, becoming such a vocal advocate that she covered the new employee with Tef-lon. The supervisor could not win. No matter what types of situations the employee would get into with the supervisor, who was very controlling and often wanted to spread bad news about the employee, the orange would mount a campaign. This orange was able to get the new employee through a rocky time, and that employee stayed at the nonprofit organization for four and a half years. That was no small feat for an office where peo-ple were often fired.

I say this to illustrate the power of the spoken word when combined with the insistence, the verve, the light in the eyes, the never-say-die attitude, the spark, the joy, the desire, the playing, the motherly love, and the sheer drive of the risk-taking, friend-making and overpowering orange. Oranges, as a group channel more energy from the divine at any given time than any of the gifts. They are the sacral chakra. This is where babies come from. I hope I don't need to say more. Yes, oranges love to say yes.

Breaking through the established way of doing things enables any orange to be themselves in joy and to do what brings them joy, which is why they must. They can all keep you, and themselves, out of hot water. Realize they know how to talk themselves out of all parking tickets. Ready and willing to connect with the divine light in the police officer, our orange friends can keep the officer from feeling that a ticket is really necessary. Some oranges feel that rules were made to be broken. Legitimate, or illegitimate, there is a line they must draw as to what they can do to bring joy. Each one must become comfortable with what they think is right and work on finding which rules to ignore. It can take them time to do so.

Sometimes, we can feel betrayed when we go along with orange plans or get involved in something they suggest, but in the end, good luck trying to stay angry with them for anything they have done. That's not easy. Because somewhere inside there you did feel good. It's up to you to decide where you needed to stand your ground and when you really needed a break from your depressing way of being. Resisting charms is impossible. They really want you to go along with them, and for good reason. It's the most fun. Yet oranges always reserve the right to say no. They say no to the things that disallow them to be in their joy, even if only temporarily. When they set something up for you, they expect you to be happy (since they are the experts on joy), and they have worked very hard (almost effortlessly) to organize and arrange a set of circumstances to bring this about. One interesting thing about this gift is that an orange may have a falling out with someone; they may even dislike someone's behavior and not want to be around them, but they will still be able to have an enjoyable time with that person and get that person to do something they want them to do. Oranges can always come back around to play the game, uplift someone, even if they have reservations about doing so at any given point.

## Orange Traps

### Staying in Unreality

Oranges in their traps might lose touch with reality. They will paint a false picture to keep their dream-reality around them. They will sometimes deny that they had anything to do with any wrongdoing. Oranges can get over an affair in a day. Externally imposed punishment and acceptance of responsibility is not an option if it doesn't feel good. When an orange acts out of love, they will have strong integrity and even so bring out the joy. Oranges are constantly connected with how they feel about themselves, the feeling in the air, and the influence of emotion on others. In their giftedness, they go with the flow in a responsible manner. They are able to follow the fun without it hurting others. In their traps, when they are not happy with the way things are going, they can manipulate people into doing the things they want them to do so they can feel good or be dishonest. This is the case when something is not done for the sake of another but rather for the orange to avoid pain. No matter how unfortunately or spectacularly they may be perceived by others, all oranges are seeking connected flow states that are characterized by 1: joy, the highest vibration, and 2: happiness, which is only possible when you "forget" the outcome. Even in our traps, we seek wisdom. We learn from our traps. Oranges do, too. If they can't find fun in their gifts, they will find it in their traps.

### Short-Term Decision Making

Oranges process a wide variety of emotions. They ride tides of emotion and will often make decisions based on their feelings. That can be okay. But larger decisions can also be based on what will bring joy later, not just now; so to delay gratification will help an orange understand that what they can accomplish is greater than short-term prosperity. When advice to others is given based on an orange's short-term feelings, that advice doesn't stand the test of time because it doesn't consider facts, wisdom, or trust in how things happen, which would create better opportunities down the road. When they give you advice based on their in-the-moment feelings, the quality of counsel goes down because how we feel does not always reflect stable reality. Sometimes they don't even stop to consider that the feeling they based a decision on resulted from their shadow side. At that juncture, an orange's feelings could be based on anything under the sun, rather than values and priorities. It's impossible to know where they're coming from when they lack judgment.

### Moving On Too Quickly, Being Unstable

While moving on is necessary for an orange, they can be too good at moving on and not finishing projects, not committing to things that could, in the end, make them more happy and bring them to greatness. The gifts and traps exist on a continuum.

When we go too far with one action, it's a trap. When we don't go far enough with another, it's a trap. It depends on the movement, the motion. Whether they are living like a social butterfly or saying yes to too many serious responsibilities, it's the same. When oranges are breathlessly reciting their lists of things to do, a trap is coming on. They get to the point where they cannot keep track of all their commitments, some of which have nothing to do with how they really feel deep inside. They are not honest. To remedy this, they need to slow down, think, and get clear on what they need to do.

### Analyzing Their Emotions and Blaming Others

One of the most serious traps an orange can get into, which hurts their inner self, is that of analyzing emotions. When they go into a situation in their mind and look for reasons why they feel the way they feel, they come up with things other people did and said that may or may not be true. When they make decisions based on the emotions that result from this story, they get off track. They avoid taking responsibility for their actions; they don't learn and they don't move on to their next steps in life. The analysis itself takes them away from their joy. They blame you because, after all, how could the joy-master cause a situation where unhappiness rules?

The belief that situations, when set up correctly, lead to happiness can catch them in a web of deceit. This happens when they've gotten attached to having things go their way because they've achieved that so many times. That's what leads to the falsification of energy, so that oranges manipulate to get what they want, instead of letting others be themselves and play the game in a fair way. Oranges can't be authentic when they're focused on trying too hard to get over emotions through making things up. Oranges in this trap will organize things so it looks like you're getting your way, then turn around and get what they want instead of you, because that's the story they're writing in their head. In the process, you may or may not get anything. They will twist and turn and turn and twist in order not to be pinned down. They want you to be over-involved and sometimes try to get you to do what they want you to do even if it won't fly.

## Self-Punishment

Oranges sometimes decide to punish themselves for the boundaries they've broken or for not being able to make something unfold in a wonderful way. But even though they can help people create joy in some dubious ways, any expression of the highest vibration is never forced but always chosen by both parties. When an orange feels joy, it's because they've successfully caused someone to choose it, not because anyone has faked anything. Even if the joy happens in an adulterated fashion, oranges got somewhere, and they aren't actually responsible if other people have regrets.

## Returning to Joy

The way out of any of these traps is to return to feeling joy within. Therefore oranges must find themselves and their divine light—but will need to change perspective or find an experience to make that happen. Because that way they won't stay stuck in their negative point of view, they'll reconnect with their soul's desires, allowing them to have fun again. Only when an orange is in their joyous state can they be the change they wish to see in others. This is where they must take the high road even when everyone else, it may seem, is taking the low one. It's necessary to keep connecting with joy even when you don't want to, even when you feel that other people show you the way to feeling bad. Being happy no matter what—breaking the connection between action and outcome—has to occur at some point in an orange's spiritual evolution. They must let themselves be happy because that is who they are, not because they focused on a circumstance to dictate it.

### Life is Like a Box of Oranges

Oranges can be great at moving on without looking back on a consistent basis. They are also among the most generous with the giving of their time, money, and energy to help you, give you counsel, and create awesome experiences of the joy-seeking variety. Oranges create joy with divine abundance. They are the joy that they seek. They are the light, they see the light, and they move toward it. They are unafraid of the power of feeling good, which some of us often forget. Still, they press on. For an orange, life is an orange, and they want you to eat it with the juice dripping down your chin.

**Famous People with an Orange Master Chakra**

Famous oranges include Mark Twain, the great American humorist, who saw humor in everything and was liked by everyone. Conan O'Brien will do anything to make you laugh, and Bob Hope helped others as a comedian and entertainer for the troops. Who in your life is an orange?

# 4

# Yellows: The Natural Thinkers

Yellows see things other people don't see because they look for light, and know that, as the *Grateful Dead* say, it's found in the strangest of places. It is because of this light they're always collecting from the shallows that they will give you a light when you have none. As a group, they have a reputation for being weird, and I mention this only because it stands as a sign of their courage to go where no one else treads; their quests bring them into contact with their true self as they become uniquely peculiar through developing their own interests. Yellows are the people who will sort through the piles of lies in Watergate to find the real truths. They want to see the truth inside the lie—and then, they will go in through the back door to get there, and develop their own beliefs, in spite of any other person's.

## Yellow Gifts

### Method and Aims

They're not looking for the darkness; they move in tune with the timing of natural cycles, with the knowledge that the earth entrusts to them, with the rhythms that natural knowing makes, because they observe nature for patterns and apply these to their experience, using them to figure out how things work. Their touch reminds you to release your pain, because they intuit where meridian points are blocked, as an acupuncturist would. They are the best at learning how to pronounce a new language, because they watch how each native speaker pronounces their words with their mouth. They both intuit and observe human beings and their ways as parts of nature—that's one of their secrets for finding out the truth. They see the connections between natural struggles and our own. For they need no books.

### A Basic Definition

People who analyze everything or always instinctively understand how to proceed with a structure that's already in place—thinking above and beyond, and who spend more time in thought than the average person—tend to be yellow. Toggling back and forth between these two forms of gaining knowledge, analyzing and gut-feeling, yellows set themselves adrift in a sea of truth-making, seeking to figure it out, collect all the facts, and find the stanchions for the foundation. Then, as well, they create a better way to help you forward. Yellows are the natural map-finders. They look for the route that you can take to get from starting point to goal, either physically, on the ground, or functionally, in another area—even spiritually. They explore, and they will eventually record in some form how to get from place to place on the journey so you do not get lost. That is why they love good books and writing comes easily to them. But if they don't prefer to stay in school, you can also find them inventing a machine. They are just as hands-on as they are philosophical.

## How They Think

Yellows automatically examine each piece of data they find to see how it fits into the whole picture they are working on completing. They work diligently either to answer your questions or to create a body of knowledge with conclusions and reasons for reaching them. While they are doing this, you may decide they are slow of wit, since they take so long. However, this is not the case. As Heidi Shelton-Oliver has observed, a yellow's mind works like a spoked wheel. So each bit of information must be followed out from the center spoke to its logical conclusion when placed side by side with the other pieces of information. It doesn't go into the making of the wheel if it hasn't been examined. The compulsion to invent a new wheel is motivated by a desire to describe "truth." And this, my friend, will answer your question—both those you asked, and those you didn't. (Usually they answer the one you really asked if they are working on your challenge, not theirs, instead of the question you thought you did.) You might want to get a good life purpose to work on while you wait for answers to ensue.

## The Definition of Truth, for Our Purposes

Truth is a contentious word in an environment where it's become increasingly volatile to discuss religion, philosophy, and politics. But that won't stop yellows from being themselves and looking for it anyway. If you have a true yellow before you, ask him or her whether she values the truth—use that language. Truth is never a dirty word for one. That's how you can tell it's their gift. Just remember that truth can be mystical, metaphorical, relative, personal, nonexistent, or absolute. It has many definitions. A yellow might add that the truth is palpable, finally clear, and stands out as the most logical answer available to us. Truth, for yellows, always has real relevance, can be applied, and will reorder experience along new lines. It will sustain you. That's its spiritual benchmark, but it's shelf-life limited. According to Joseph Crane, it's a vehicle, not a destination. Truth is trust in things unseen, and that's why many people don't like the word. It's truth that finally lays bare what is really going on. But those who arrive at the station of truth know it in their being, because they feel the accord they have and hold with what stabilizes in their soul as being real. Mountains of evidence can be given to back it up, and all of that evidence is findable by a yellow. This is why we can trust their conclusions when they're ready to give them to us.

Information that comes after an accepted truth will change it and make it new. Therefore, truth is an answer to a question that is most nearly correct given the information that is known at the time. It is a constellation of facts that have connections to create a whole picture. Yellows search for something that frees human beings from constraint, and this is the truth they want you to know about and use to make your life better and keep you safe from harm (in survivalist, poignant terms).

## Mr. Snowden

Edward Snowden, high-school dropout and whistle-blower for the National Security Agency's surveillance program, which collects metadata both at home and for the US government around the world, uses classic yellow soul-ray methods to find the truth. His most basic approach is the use of his self-taught own mind. Yellows are curious and seek the truth as a matter of course. With a community-college computer education, Snowden was suspected of trying to break into classified files while an employee for the CIA. He then took a job as a contractor, and from there he gathered evidence that the US was spying on foreign countries and its own citizens alike. (Yellows always find a way in when denied access.) It's difficult to find one who doesn't feel disturbed by the fact that our laws are either not being followed or are erroneously written. They want to hold onto, and keep undisturbed, pathways to truth, and when those are violated (such as the constitution), they perceive that everyone is endangered. If you were in charge of finding ways for people to live good lives, wouldn't you feel an injustice was being done if they were threatened? All interviews with Mr. Snowden show a detached, yet warm and curious person interested in protecting the public good. Like all yellows, he shares the details incessantly on what he's discovered, and knows seventeen different ways to get around security. He changes his mind, questions his decisions, takes a long time to perform simple tasks (because he's paying attention to every detail), yet always comes back to the idea that a massive compromise of security is a good enough cause to become a refugee for. He's a yellow's yellow, of the golden soul-ray.

## Neutrality

Because if we had no one who could remove their emotion from a belief system, get past their own desires long enough to answer a question on a formal basis, take a neutral point of view, and defend the truth (not to mention deliver it), then we would have a much harder time trusting our decisions that they lead from a foundation of actuality, reality, and feasibility. Asking too many questions about everyday things and making a treasure hunt out of a problem to be solved that most people think for two minutes about are symptoms of a person who uses stoicism to encounter the divine. Yellows reach the top because they are smart and they use their own form of scientific method, which consists of staying skeptical for far longer than most others would, and figuring out all aspects of a topic. I do, however, advocate truth with a heart.

### Solving Your Problems, One by One

If not by inventing things, they bring you solutions. Yellows work out how you could successfully diet, how to surgically repair the arteries leading to the heart, how to travel to work bipedally. They tell you which is the best dumpster to rent and what the best bike shoes are. And if they can't find the best bike shoes, they'll invent a new pair. They do it because the design isn't functional enough. A yellow is always more concerned with content above form. But eventually, form will come into the mix as a matter of course. They are wily like a cat. They follow a cowpath to show where the knowledge leads, taking you with them. They have a clean energy, one of innocence, not experience, and one of ultimate distraction. Though their non-conformity is bold, their manner is tidy. Though their striving is hard, they make it look easy. Never be fooled by a yellow. They eventually come through. It might take them years, eons. But like water smooths rocks, eventually their hard edges give out as they work out their sums. Eventually they come to be seen as the one who knows. The result of all their problem-solving experience can be stunning, such as the story of a woman I know who worked on an assembly line with no college degree and landed herself in the engineering department because she could figure out how to make better parts.

### Releasing Thought from Emotion

To see how yellows stay nonemotional when they are coming up with their truth, let's take a moment to consider what the word emotion means. Emotion refers to a circumstance that creates a feeling. Emotions are multivarious movements of energy that thoughts bring with them. Like a hand fan, they extend in finite directions from a spectrum of motion in time and space. They consist of the reactions, responses, and behaviors someone has while perceiving a situation. What yellows are able to do is hold at bay such responses to individual thoughts while they are cross comparing and assembling them together. What they are working on is completing a holographic picture and don't consider one building block to be any better than any another. All facts are equal, they say. In fairness, consider all facts.

They take three times as long as we think they will. That's how yellows can't afford to explore each emotion attached to every thought they capture, because if they did, they'd get too overloaded with the consequences of each thought. Since they are not bringing to a close, or a conclusion, their thought process in a fast manner, they know innately they can afford to wait on emotion while they've put all the pieces together to come to a firm conclusion. Some people find extricating themselves from emotion easier to do than others—it all depends on how in touch with your solar-plexus chakra you are, or how well you've developed this energy center both now and in past lifetimes. But suffice to say, yellows do it best because their soul ray gently implores them to do so, granting them the clarity and peace of mind to do so. Yellows unfold truth. Their lives stand the test of time as expressions of truth's exploration and logical conclusions, as lived out in their minds.

## Mr. Exact

One of my strongest yellow examples is known among family friends as "Mr. Exact." Once I asked him to do a cleansing process according to some unusual directions—at a time when the sun was at its highest point in the sky. While everyone else had always assumed this was noon, Mr. Exact consulted sources to discover when the sun was at its highest point, and it turned out to be 12:31 p.m. Yellows do not take things at face value, they go and investigate. They investigate little things because they adore small jobs. Looking for the pathway to truth starts on the ground, with details.

## The Humor of Taking Things Literally

Since yellows are always paying attention to details, valuing each and every one, it can be hard for them to get jokes. They will try to figure out what you've said, and not get it. What they value like cash is a specific form of humor that plays on words in the incongruous. They often don't get other types of jokes because they are built to take things seriously in order to process and analyze. Literal humor, though, is the humor of *Spaceballs*, where you see strawberry jam smeared on a spaceship hurtling through space, because there is a jam in the machine. Yellow's favorite jokes are those like the one with a headline stating "Inbred Cat" over a picture of a cat with its head sticking out of a piece of bread. Double meanings, anything that juxtaposes the literal world with the rest of the world—can be imposed as truth or dare. A game? A game of tricks, a game of life. Usually, I come to remind my yellow friends to stop taking things literally. When they take you literally, sometimes you have to learn lessons. It will force you to do things that you never thought you would do.

## Yellow Traps

Like all the master chakras, yellow have traps that describe how they act when their egos are in charge. In those places, yellows expect you to believe their conclusions and to follow them in lockstep, which can lead to a trap of manipulation, where they expect you to think and play their game their way (because they are the ones who are right). Once someone no longer wants to participate in the pinball game of trying to follow the yellow rabbit down into the hole and through the warren in the dark, and not getting to think for themselves, a line has been crossed. As with all traps, there can be a gray area where we are not sure whether or not someone is in a trap—whether ego is too dominant or not dominant enough, or whether the person is motivated to act for the good of all. Circumstance dictates this.

### Confusion

The most serious root trap, outside emotional coldness, is schlepping facts and truths but not collecting them into a whole body of knowledge that can be understood and communicated to others. Leaving all the Lego pieces in a mess on the floor interminably will not help anyone, least of all this master chakra. In these times, to get organized, to refocus, to reconnect with natural knowing, and to connect to reason is the best thing to do. Not working toward collected truth that makes sense and keeping everything up in the air won't help anyone. This makes a yellow scattered and unfocused. When confusion abounds in your world because of them, they are in their traps. Remember, these are the clarity-bringers. They need time to do it, but you should feel a sense of freedom, not debris. We all have this when we look at the state of our solar plexus chakra. Either it can do the functions of truth-seeking effectively, or it's in a state of chaos where we don't believe in ourselves and trust ourselves even less.

## Passivity

Sometimes, immovability, or passivity, is a trap. They will tell you something cannot be improved—that if you are married, don't get divorced—and if you are not married, don't get married. That point of view, in itself, is not a trap—it's typical yellow thinking, which they get from their green side: preserve the structure if it doesn't cost you a lot of energy to do so. If it's the fastest way to get from point A to point B, they will recommend the status quo. But if yellows get stuck in rigidity, it's a danger zone. The trap-like state is refusing to change their mind (not to say that they don't change it too much in their traps, as well). If the winds are really blowing, and they need to go to a new place in their life in order to advance, then it's time to let down the guard, feel emotions, and proceed with new life. It is a yellow who knows the truth and won't change, even after they know better, that really irks me and is the reason I'm writing this book. They are all about preservation, recommending the surgical strike. Still, when they get lost in confusion, don't wrap things up or get pieces in line for a conclusion, or even just a transition, they can neither know nor clearly share what is true.

## *Unavailable Emotionally*

Yellows will stuff emotions, cordoning them off so they cannot be reached, and withdraw from society. They are supposed to keep emotion out of analysis. However, they must not keep emotions out of life. On their trap-side, they don't see the usefulness of emotions. They can read too many emotions as inappropriate, and thus, those very same emotions tend to become inappropriate when finally expressed. Not only that, but they can fail to relate to others emotionally when it's really necessary to keep a relationship going. They give you the cold shoulder.

Yellows feel that knowledge is a point of view, and they stick to that. Because ultimately, they are right. They will insist on holding points of view that others do not if it fits what they see is the best, most solid position to command. And because they are so committed to the truth, they can hold onto such a point of view in spite of gale-force winds. Only a new truth can dissuade them, and only when they are open to receive it. Mostly, they are open, but when their emotional box gets triggered and they explode, or implode, then they are not open. Sometimes they try not to be emotional out of malice. Other times they lose control over their emotions because they go unexpressed for so long.

### Communication Skills with No Finesse

While not explicitly a trap, delivering the truth too bluntly verges on being a trap if it entails a history of suppressed emotion. (How else could the person learn to be impolite in the first place, if they didn't repress their human feelings?) Traps are places we mess up, where we need to watch our actions. Yellows stuck in their traps can always use communication skills. They can always use more compassion and understanding. No one ever told me that a yellow was too heart-centered. No one ever told me that he or she was too loving, too kind, or too rational. The brain can use a letdown to the heart chakra. Yellows can use their supple, flexible side to reach people if they keep the big picture in mind when speaking to them, feeling in their heart what is necessary before saying what they have to say. When it comes to a yellow, "the truth will out," as they say. And probably more often than not. The question here is: how will it be stated? This is a blue concern, but it needs to be addressed since so many yellows alienate through lack of delivery, when a good number of others knock the ball out of the park with it.

The reason that there are more yellow men on dating websites than any other color is because they spend too much time in their heads, in their traps, and they neglect the emotional side of life. Women who are yellow tend to be more in touch with emotions because it's more socially acceptable to be that way. Yet all yellows I encounter as a spiritual advisor usually need to be encouraged to feel their feelings. It can go a long way toward helping them interact better with others.

## Taking Too Long a Journey

Yellows do not always live in the world of reality. They can fail to connect a present circumstance with the idealism in their heads, and they don't pick up actions they need to take. Cases of yellow children who don't turn in their homework because they are not finished yet are common. In these cases, the child chooses to get a zero instead of risk a B, not because they don't care about grades, but because they care about the quality of their work, and it's not quality until they've worked on it enough. They can take a long time to complete their projects, but they need to consider the timelines of others as well and fit their schedules to the realm of reason and timing.

## Doubting Truth

After working so hard on a research project, whether it stays in their heads, finds its way to press, or becomes an object of curiosity (an experiment) to show everyone, you wouldn't think yellows would doubt the end of the road when it's near. Still, in a trap-like state, they cannot stop questioning, even after their conclusion has been proven sound. In order for yellow information to be good, it must be delivered timely (for a yellow—but not too long) and then they must believe it! And then, act on it, but not in a pie in the sky way. It's a delicate balance, to work with all these elements and keep them streamlined. They must accept their own truth: that is the final challenge.

### Cliffhanger

What do yellows do with all the data they collect? They store it in their minds. The metadata that the government collects is just one big yellow mind, which the tiny yellow mind of Edward Snowden accessed. Yellows find the most relevant facts by sifting through every last line of computer code, but it doesn't have to take them a long time, as in the following story.

"Once when I was rock-climbing, I slipped down a few feet and was barely grabbing onto rock, holding my entire body weight up while slipping off. My friend was at the top of the cliff, and after a while, when we could see no way out, started to shut down, knowing I would die. He was already crying and acting like I was dead. I didn't know what to do. All of a sudden, my mind brought forth a word. It was a word that came from the primordial soup of humanity, somehow from the farthest reaches of my mind, clawing its way through the depths of my psyche, breaking water like a deep-sea diver, and that word was mommy. I remembered all the times I was safe with my mommy when I was baby, naked on her chest, nestling in her breasts, and my hand reached up to grab something, and it went into the exact spot where there was a knob of rock and I could hang onto to pull myself up, and that was how I finally was able to heave myself up over the cliff."

This example really shows how a yellow reads the natural world, and communicates with it, to find the best paths to follow. Not only did the Universe motivate this person with an experience that might want to make him save his life, the experience (of breasts) paralleled the knob of rock he grabbed to save himself. That is so yellow! It's safe to say that most yellows live dangerously, whether physically or mentally. It's hard for me to think of examples of yellows where they weren't cruising off a cliff like the Fool in the tarot card deck, totally innocent, hobo bag in tow, ready for the next adventure. Both mental and physical progress is really the same, for them, in the end, because to question common knowledge, as we have seen in our examples so far, is to place yourself on the edge of embodied experience, pushing the envelope. While it can take them a long time to think things through, as they question everything, the linkability of their data is legion, and they can touch one piece of it to get the answer they need instantly.

## An Answer's Impact

What helps guide yellows in their research is their spiritual sources—the environment of our experience; their "natural" knowing, their core consciousness to "just" know; these abilities allow them to engage all factors in a search for truth in an even-handed way. Once they tell you their answer to your question, short or long, it may not be what you expected to hear—and sometimes, you won't want to hear it. Especially when something was your fault, because you were negligent in some area, and then certain things failed to take place. When life doesn't work how you thought it would, yellows have a talent for sharing in an off-hand way, sometimes through a question alone, truth that sets you free. But there are times when it will almost kill you to hear it. That truth that a yellow so easily came upon, that perspective they spent years gathering, sounds devastating to you because you weren't built to perceive as they perceive, so their perceptions can be arresting. But like so many of us, even yellows can want to run when the going gets tough. The truth is not an easy talk to walk.

While some yellows are better than others at softening your experience of the truth they find, others will just give you their truth as they see it and wonder why you're dismayed. The best thing about this gift is it bows to no emotion in its answer, in its time, in its substance. This is why a yellow's information is considered "foundational." It is their knowledge on which we can build wisdom, love, joy, healing, talent, and all our fine arts. If we let it.

## Famous People with a Yellow Master Chakra

An example of a famous yellow is Leonardo Da Vinci; he was constantly observing the natural world to find the truth of how things worked, activating his natural knowing and bringing analysis to bear upon it in order to convey this. He rejected any knowledge that did not grow out of one's own observation of the world. A typical yellow, he did not need books to do research. He recorded all of his research in his notebooks and drawings and used this knowledge to invent things. He was an engineer and philosopher; for him, art was a medium of research and shared knowledge.

Another famous yellow is the character Sheldon from *The Big Bang Theory*. He has unique interests and moved to the top of his field due to his thought process. Sheldon always uses his mind to search for the truth and makes decisions based on fact. He's not afraid of appearing unconventional. Can you find the yellows in your life? What makes them yellow?

# 5

# GREENS: THE
# NATURAL FIXERS

Greens are the fixers. Also known as the "healers," they bring things back into balance. For greens, finding solutions to problems and applying them, doing the physical work of "fixing," is their life's blood, and when it really comes down to it, they do like to fix things, as opposed to people. But to fix something requires many other skills: discernment, knowledge of the problem, options, best solutions, how to apply those solutions, and an understanding of maintenance.

Greens focus first on what needs to be fixed, instead of the people who might doubt them. They work through the stuff that contributes in some way usefully even in the midst of their dysfunction. They are not perfectionistic, though many are. They are drawn first and foremost to focus with their master chakra on the deeper layers of what needs to be fixed "about" a person, rather than viewing the person as someone they can't change, or seeing their life as off-limits. It doesn't make any sense to a green that a person would want to keep the things holding them back—unless they are stuck in their traps.

Greens take the exactitude of yellow and apply it to their interests—using data to create a balance and create a process for keeping things in balance. Because they want to do things a specific, particular way, they are looking for an extension of truth— a solution to their problem that entails the truth about how things work, and work together. Their interest in making things work together and knowing how things work together well is how greens teach us balance. They bring us "reason" because they want things to work well in the physical world; they can't be up in the clouds to accomplish such a task. Their interest in making things work together well is how greens learn to become trusted in the realm of working with people. They want reasonable standards to apply to everything they do. Their desiring that everything function optimally in the physical world is a result of their focus on grounding with clarity.

But don't be fooled. Greens are reasonable, not entirely logical. They do not care to explain what is happening all the time, for they can't. There is too much mysticism going on for them in their journey toward finding solutions to issues, though analysis may be ongoing. Who can say exactly what and why they did what they did? Who can say how they knew how to fix the broken drill or find a creative solution to the curtain rod issue. It is a mystery, one known only to a green. This group is not called a "healer" for nothing. There are too many doorways open into the beyond, and the beyond of the beyond, for them to really clearly know how they got their efficient fix. So even though they can analyze what will work best, that is not their featured resonance. Rather, they find more depth and worth in the subconscious mind, and feeling into spirit, for what will really make them fly. Focusing on how things work is not the same as knowing how things work.

## Green Gifts

*Energy as Medium*

Greens see everything as energy, and this is what they want to bring into balance, the stuff behind the stuff. This energy can appear in different forms—it can be subtle energy or energy already formed into something in the world you can touch and see. How energy works and flows is what greens are in touch with through nature's pathways into the mysterious. They love nature and sense how nature heals; they use these healing patterns in their work. Therefore, while things grow in stages, not everything comes first, second, third, and fourth in a line, as we like to expect. Greens do not go in a straight line in pursuit of wisdom. They do not choose the straight lines that other humans may have set up, especially if those other humans were not green. They might put the cart before the horse. Things are circular and cyclical, and greens are one with this "mood" of nature, of woman, and of the right side of the body, when they are healing something or bringing it into balance. They can be very structured on the one hand and very surreal in their process of creation on the other, going into dreamlike states to see what can be revealed of the energies of the universe.

Did I mystify you? If you couldn't exactly understand with logic what I just said, then you have entered the green world. Fixing is a process of renewal, often of rebirth. Greens must access the feminine, even though their gift is masculine, in order to manifest their solutions.

Their work with energy puts them in close touch with money in a way unlike any other gift. Unlike any other gift, money does not have to be a loaded word for a green. Greens see money as just another thing that is in our world for us to manage. It doesn't have the deep mystique, or the fear, that it can hold for some. For greens, money is an energy, and it too must balance. This practical relationship with money leads them to save, not spend.

They are very dispassionate when balancing the books. They see your money, if they are managing it, like a bucket, and they don't want any holes in it. You must stop punching a hole in it. They will not like it. They will save your money and not give it back to you. They will not acknowledge checks in the mail. They are either money in the bank or not yet in existence. Greens are black and white when it comes to energy management. They, like reds, are good at setting boundaries. Instead of looking at what belongs to whom, they look at what is and what is not.

### The Body of Love

Because of their deep appreciation and striving for balance, they are very strong; they feel they must stay strong for others. They shift energies around so that they can help others and create a safe, calm space. This is the healing space. That is who they are. Still, peaceful. You will know a green by this energy, for they exude calm. They are the trunk of the tree, the middle of the chakra system with three chakras on one side, three on the other—evenly balanced: the fulcrum point.

As we know, when something goes out in one area, a factor in a corresponding area is normally affected. Even if things are going haywire, they are serious about focusing your energy and being on track with that task. They are kind, loving from here—after they have helped you. While they are looking for solutions, they hold themselves apart. This is the healing space. So greens are constantly striving to weave a tapestry of their work together as a balanced whole. Balance is a moving target. They pull on those threads from multiple directions to create a space in which people can thrive, an objective that makes sense to the world and works for all involved. Therefore, they must access the stillness of creation, the beingness that connects you to the heartbeat of all. They can achieve oneness in their peaceful state and pass it on to others. If you need to be still, for things not to be weird, to be comfortable in your own body, sit next to a green.

They tend to look at anything blocked and out of balance as a new center where there could be calmness and stillness instead of disarray. They are drawn to the center of the problem so that they can plant a tree of strength there and have the branches support the rest of life … this is how they go right to the middle of a problem, by imagining themselves there and taking note of everything that is a part of the problem. They want to move the fewest branches of support that they need to in order to bring everything back into place. However, if they have to redo the entire castle you built, they will. If they have to advise you to turn your life upside down in order to achieve balance in one significant area, many will not hesitate to use any means at their disposal to ensure that it happens.

Greens are in charge of bringing so much of our environment into balance, and this leads them to being critical in order to get us to pay attention to what is going on around us. We need to wake up. We don't see where we are hurting ourselves. When a green walks into a room, a forest, or enters a website, they see what is in need of repair. This master chakra cannot help but tell you about it. Greens are always talking about what needs to be upgraded or fixed; when greens talk, it is in the mode of process, how things are in process, why, and where they are going. They are always seeing potential for improvement and adjustment to move things back into precision. Some people do not like this kind of criticism, and some greens have learned, whereas others have not, how to state what must be done with love and ensure what they say is constructive. Some greens make most of their conversation about what has gone wrong, while others do not. However, most greens discuss process and problems and how things work as a matter of course, because that is how they enlighten the rest of us to the awareness behind their eyes.

### Pandora's Toolbox

They are masters at putting things back together once they have the right tools. This is why they love tools. These tools could come in the form of information and knowledge, or as actual equipment. The right tools can be used with the right standard operating procedures (SOPs). Greens have a natural knack for putting things together. They usually go about their lives using tools in the context of solutions and SOPs. That's another thing that makes their gift masculine: the structure they proceed with once they've visited the feminine for answers.

When they come up with the best systems to keep in balance the things needing to be done, not everyone wants to go along with them at all times, as we saw in the orange chapter. Greens are so creative, though, that they can build what they cannot find prefabricated and insert people into their game plan as though they are tools themselves. This is where a gray area comes into being and where a trap might arise.

So, in their traps, greens can suddenly make people into tools. The traps of every master chakra consist of the person turning their gift into something that is done for selfish reasons. In this sense, traps are not bad, yet they hold less love. It's when people become tools merely used by the green to carry out their vision, and not for the benefit of others, that causes harm. Other times it may go unnoticed or not be a big deal.

Though their view of money is very healthy, greens can be greedy in their traps. This means they just want more. They don't care how they get it, because people become the means to an end, not living beings to love and honor. And in this sense, greens can be very uncaring.

## Loyal Persistence

In general, greens in their gifts are often more compassionate and loyal—because they are process-oriented—than they are effusively loving and kind, in the traditional sense. If they are loving and kind, it is coming from their personality. Having the pulse of universal energy has them returning their focus to the "stuff" of life. They will spend a lot of time helping you, and they are willing to give a tremendous amount of energy to see that things happen in the way they want.

Greens take the information that others give them and they discover and apply it to create a workable solution. Each cog in the wheel must function precisely, however, so don't expect just any solution to seem acceptable to a green right away. No sentiment will be used in place of reason. Greens immediately recognize when something will help them solve the problem, but they can also be cautious and skeptical about it, because they can also see how it might *not* work.

After seeing a green do some editing, I was amazed at how easily the person saw the most efficient way to move words around to make a better sentence. It was as if she was able to know the best way to go about fixing the sentence using some sort of magic. People notice the magical. Greens pull things out of the air, and to me, it always seems like they see things in the following way, in an interconnected series of ellipses.

There are all these pieces that somehow connect, and they know—and use—that knowing to apply a "fix." Like all colors, you don't have to be an expert in a certain area to be able to offer something in the way of your gift to it. There are tasks that crave experts and tasks that do not. Here, we are talking about natural expertise and how we can draw on that for many more purposes than we previously thought we could. Therefore, if you need something fixed, consider a green—and if you need someone with definite expertise, consider a green in that line of work.

## The Case of the Illiterate Mechanic

I once knew a green with very poor reading skills who managed to hold a good job as a mechanic because he could look at pictures and intuit how cars worked. When I was his literacy coordinator, for a gift, he gave me a combination tool that was a solar, hand-crank emergency radio, flashlight, cell phone charger. Like most greens, he wanted to be prepared for anything.

Because of the mystical nature of their process, not all greens are verbally adept. Some have trouble expressing themselves lyrically because they don't work in a linear fashion. Others are just fine in that area and can be eloquent. While they want to tell you about the SOPs they set up for you, they don't necessarily want to tell you how they know or arrived at all their information. They usually do not want to tell you more than they need to, and they also love to work alone. Having people watch them work is very disagreeable. They do not want to headline a conference. They want to sit in the back row. If they do headline the conference, they will be very prepared. They will never give you all the information that you crave; that is a blue's job.

When a green is in her traps, she may break something just to be able to fix it. Or she may see something that does not have a problem but claim it does. This is because greens can't help but look for things to fix; it is an inborn drive. (Did I say that already?) So sometimes, they make it up. They will not quit. They do not know when enough is enough, when "perfect" means it's okay the way it is. They will go on and on about something wrong that is not wrong. The extension of this trap is not believing things are perfect just as they are, because they are. The word *perfect* means "meets the standard." So, everything is perfect. There will always be more to clean, organize, and balance. So in order to have balance in their own lives and not have to be strong for everyone all the time, greens must perfect the art of seeing perfection in messiness and allow chaos to be beautiful.

### Meaningful Fixing
Loral Langemeier is an example of a green who helps the world through her gift by shifting people's livelihoods into balance.

She fixes people's businesses that are not successful or even off the ground yet and makes them successful. She does so by putting in place a sequence of steps that one must take, priorities they must follow, to enable people to succeed. She has organized a system that encourages you to organize your business in a certain way to make money—again the natural province of a green. To a green, money is good because it supports life. Without life, we have no experience of anything. Money is very important and must be accounted for, taken seriously, and above all, made and safeguarded. Money is the blood in the system of the body we call society—and ultimately, it's that body greens are interested in working on and making work the best it can. Of course they do it best when doing it from the heart.

Honoring a green's gift means accepting their ongoing critique of how things are and their striving to make them whole by not only fixing them in the short term but putting in place the best way to do things for the long term. You can help greens by accepting their gift and also knowing when you feel that things are good enough. Greens process the world in terms of what's going on that might be threatening to the rest of us. At heart, they strive to keep us out of danger—to prevent the upset of things that we need to keep us safe (a good toaster), in balance (a healthy body), and in harmony with the rest of the world (a take-no-prisoners 100% natural face cream.)

## *Their Nature*

By nature, greens love to clean and organize. This is part of creating the physical space that supports healing, so it's no wonder. They also love to dress sharply, since nothing is left to chance in the forward progress of helping things take their best form. They are spiritual to the core, and through them, we see that God likes to have his stuff together. They tend to be sensitive—or tough as nails. They give you tough love. They will get you the help you need, and that means you'll experience pain. They'll sit with you while you feel pain, very unsympathetically, while not flinching. They want to see the healing come about, and hold space for you while that happens. They care most for you by caring that you shift. If they were afraid of pain, they might not be able to stand setting your bones.

## Green Traps

In their traps, greens face the darkness like all of the other gifts. Instead of healing others out of love, they become overly focused on the process of fixing, and they can even stop caring whether or not the patient is failing. Getting power from fixing someone or something is very beguiling. A lot of people notice when a green fixes something. They get kudos. When someone else admires what they do and were born to do too much, they can get cocky, like a doctor who can do no wrong. And we do admire doctors—because they can fix us, and we are not sure exactly how they do it.

Not knowing when to quit is a green trap. Not knowing when enough is enough—when the person is recovered, when the disease is in remission, when we are in balance—is a lack of perspective that can come from being drunk on one's own power. It is a form of greed.

Greed is also a green trap as it relates to power and money. Always needing more money, to save every penny, even of others' money, can be greedy if it is self-serving. When greens want the best for others, on the other hand, they emerge from this trap.

Greens will never stop noticing when something needs to be fixed; they do need to learn realistic boundaries around such. Not everything can and will be fixed on a fast timeline. Being very dissatisfied and crotchety is a likely state of being for a green who refuses to see things as perfect even when the dishes have been dirty for a week.

In some settings, it is totally legitimate to want other people to do things in certain ways so that a solution comes to pass. But slipping toward "solving the problem at any price" is where the trap falls. Ends-justify-the-means thinking is easy for a green to slip into because they focus on the things, the items, the stuff of life. They focus on things as objects. It's too easy to make people some of those objects when we are only human and we've practiced solving exacting solutions all of our life. Greens, more than any other color, have vested interest in having things go right, process-wise. The reason this behavior can land on the dark side is because it can ignore people's self-determination and right to be their own person and right to be perfect as-is, if that is what they choose. Being overly critical is, therefore, a green trap. It is all about balance.

Mature greens find ways to communicate their observations of the world in ways that allow people to be themselves, without leading with critique so as to annoy people. Another characteristic of someone who is mature in their gift of green is that they allow others privacy—they do not pry. A prying green is an unwanted green, and greens tend to experience loneliness from people leaving them when they conduct their power as an extension of themselves instead of as a gift from God. Like all of us, greens can choose the higher self versus the ego at any time. Sometimes one is appropriate, sometimes another—however, out-of-control ego, or "getting drunk on their own power," is the real essence of the trap. The ego can be used in healthy ways by greens, too. So, to be safe, greens need to remind themselves that they should look to their own divine source as the facilitator of all of their healing gifts, and then they will come into balance again.

They may have a great many ideas for how to do things in the best manner, but they use our humble, current systems to promote wellness, and if those systems don't work well enough for us, they fix them, either through what they do, or how they do it. They want to manage how you do what you do, because if only you follow their correct procedures, you will see results beyond your wildest dreams.

*Divine Glory Their Focus*

For many greens, their feelings about a situation, in the way that it is, are divinely inspired. Their matter-of-fact manner and their choices give them away. As they experience it, God works through them effortlessly, in a down-to-earth, timeless way to ensure that their humanity and sanity, in their human body, delivers divine connection and worth. This who they are: the mind, the heart, the hands of God and Goddess, the female and male aspects of God, which together form a whole. It's characterizes all of us at times, but in them it operates with less obfuscation, because they approach things so organically while still being direct and to the point with the mind. This group is not called to be healers for nothing. The doorway opens wide, the threshold appears; and that's when a green will clearly know they've arrived at a stunning conclusion. Analysis assists in this process, it doesn't replace it. The numinous follows them wherever they go, but strikes them without warning. Consider that in addition to purple, greens have the most love, even though this isn't necessarily followed by an emotional closeness, as it is with that other color. You experience more of who God is when you experience these two colors in their gifts.

## Famous People with a Green Master Chakra

Famous greens include Martha Stewart (creating peace and calm in the home with the exact tools and look) and Bob Vila (original host of *This Old House*, who is a master Mr.-fix-it). Who are the greens of your world? What characteristics show that they exhibit this gift?

# 6

# BLUES: THE NATURAL TEACHERS

Natural teachers educate. *Educere* means to "draw out from within" or "lead forth," which is what a teacher will do with anyone, if they have access. A person with a blue master chakra peers into you and points out the information you have and mixes it with new information they know or have. In doing so, they want produce wisdom, or the application of knowledge. They will often surprise others by knowing their thoughts, but the teacher must know what a student knows if they are to add anything of value. Equally automatically, people on the blue ray have what other people need to know to develop their knowledge on a subject more in depth. It's always true that a blue won't always be able to tell you why or how they know. They just know, and they know that they know. They receive messages from the divine and deliver them without stopping to question their content, validity, or any feelings the listener might have. Blues need to feel, however, that they can or should trust their knowings, if they don't. Because understanding the missing pieces of a conversation is a gift they are given from God, and it's good, even if it's not easy to trace every piece of that information they receive. Blues fill in the gaps of other people's awareness so they experience the relief of having development on topics that were in need of growth, so the person can be ready for their next steps.

## Blue Gifts

### Making Connections

As a rule, blues are drawn to illuminate concepts and discuss the connections with who you are. The root of their approach is based on connections among pieces of knowledge, betwixt all people, and between student and teacher. You become their student once you've decided to listen. Natural teachers can be recognized because they are drawn to make connections between things people say. They illuminate the ties between different pieces of information from the past, present, and the future, and from seemingly unrelated sources or subjects. They use thoughts from their own knowledge base and information they download from the divine in structuring their connections. They connect the people they know with each other, and give books, music, opportunities, references, and referrals, or anything at all that can help that person develop into a better human being. Blues exuberantly give what they give to others because they see potentials in people. They speak to their light—that's part of how they enlighten. It's all to create a better, stronger connection, but one that can mutually transform and enlighten so we can move ahead.

Blues want to see humanity advance. In groups and individually, they play the role of imparting information in order to weave together what people say. They are good translators of ideas from one person to another. If someone in a group setting does not understand something, they are very good at clarifying the information. Blues want to talk, talk, talk; that is their primary teaching method. Very quiet blues have mostly suppressed their throat chakra desires to share what is in their heart, on their mind, and just waiting to be channeled through them to free someone's soul. They can practice doing so, however.

People receive enlightenment from blues, which means they literally receive more light as a result of talking with them. When blues are teaching, they make nonjudgmental statements that sound like facts, which is how they deliver all of their information and perceptions. The manner of the teacher is one of impartiality, confidence, and structure. The blue master chakra is mentally assumptive. It doesn't seek the truth, per se, it assumes the truth in what it acknowledges, observes, and knows. Like yellows, blues don't have to do research, because they receive their knowledge from a source they don't question. However, research can expand and unwrap a blue's true powers of sharing things that others will find useful. Blues do like to seek out information that can help someone grow. They love helping people be the best they can be. Blues are amenable to research.

## Balanced Between Masculine and Feminine

Blues embody balance in their gifts, because they always want to walk with wisdom, and you have to know that two sides of a whole are one to really see the deep truths of life. They don't see why they shouldn't be masculine as much as they are feminine, and vice versa. They use their masculine side to seed knowledge, but their feminine side to affirm knowledge and nurture what they teach. When blues teach, they move back and forth from masculine to feminine points of view. They strive to satisfy the directives of opposites. Here are two examples of blues, one of whom was focused on doing her gift without stopping, and the other who found balance in simply being himself. In our masculine, we focus on doing. In our feminine, we focus on how to be.

## Judy

Like a dreamer, Judy had her head firmly planted in the clouds, and her feet only touched the soil to help absorb new understandings. My best blue spiritual teacher, Judy looked to the sky for ideas. She did not walk in the land of dust. She took in the spiritual world constitutionally; it made her stronger. She learned everything she could learn and discussed it at length. She joined every program, read every book, every blog post, every manual, and listened to every podcast she could get her hands on in the subjects she was interested in. While I would tire of gaining new teachings, since I always felt I needed to work hard to apply them, Judy felt no such compulsion and simply ate up more, like a Pac-Man eats dots. If there was a new metaphysical angle that could shed new light on life, she wanted it. Then, she shared it with her friends and clients when a problem came up. She not only flew to one of my three-day workshops from five states away, she brought a friend. Out of all the soul-rays, people with a blue master chakra have the most endurance, and Judy always impressed me with her breadth and depth of knowledge—she had the will and the control to receive spiritual teachings from disparate corners and synthesize them into her own philosophy, which she turned on you like a fire hose to clean away all that dirt and dust from the world—which results from too hard of a focus on gaining material status, money, and power, instead of caring for your soul. *That* she couldn't tolerate. She was grounded, but not in the earth most of us know. Bridging the spiritual and the mental is what blues do best. Judy took from the spiritual and communicated it in the mental realm to anyone who would listen. She was a walking, talking throat chakra.

## John

John was a spiritual person who always told you what he thought and didn't care what other people thought. He got tired of people doing things in the same way. A blue master chakra will consider the past for the sake of the future. They don't stay stuck in it. It's important that a person grows. John felt that the old Christian ways were worn out. He was a disabled person, and he felt that they could disable his soul if he continued to look to them. He felt there were newer, lighter things to focus on. Connecting to the past is good when it entails enlightenment, but for him, the light was gone in his church, and he wouldn't attend anymore—he knew that he himself was a church, the church of Philadelphia. Blue master chakra lights don't want to stay where the light has been mostly dimmed, and this is why they always stay on the cutting edge of all new thought, not just in spirituality, but in other fields, like John did with his new age perspectives.

### Balanced In All Four Bodies

Blues constantly seek balance in their own lives because it helps them stay in spiritual alignment. Enlightening people entails lining them up with Source, so that they pursue physical, mental, emotional, and spiritual paths simultaneously. This is another area where blues want to stay ahead of the game. They can't line other people up with God if they can't line up themselves. So, they want stimulating conversation, emotional context, physical activity, and spiritual learning. They look to gain knowledge from each area regularly so that they don't feel off. They feel best when they can be themselves, and it's what allows them to teach and be heard.

## Contrary Teaching Tools

Another characteristic trait is speaking in opposites. In their giftedness, a person on the blue ray likes to bring forward aspects in a conversation that have not been looked at yet. Sometimes it's directly opposite what is being expressed. "On the other hand," or "in addition" are favorite sentence-starters for the teacher. They are driven to bring forward always one more aspect of the issue at hand, normally contrary, to enlighten you, not to be belligerent. This is because for a teacher, everything is what it is not. Teachers do not hold tightly to what they say or hold themselves to behave in tandem with what they say. *That* they consider bondage. This is because they are devil's advocates, and what they say is always an outgrowth of the moment and context in which they are working. Teachers have values and convictions, for sure, but their words are aimed toward shining a light for you on what you must notice right now—and what is true right now. That might change in the next moment. Therefore, sometimes teachers can seem to have a shifting set of values, goals, and advice for you and themselves. They can seem to live in the world of opposites. If a natural teacher were to try to stop themselves from being a devil's advocate, it would be the equivalent of taping their mouth shut.

## Listening

Blues strive to speak without holding back because of conventions, censorship, or other people's feelings. What is improper to one person might not offend your blue friend. Blues just don't get offended like others, because for them, any subject is a topic with merit to be discussed, and can be discussed impersonally on some level. Therefore, they will answer embarrassing questions about themselves without getting embarrassed. They know you must need to know, or you wouldn't have asked.

Blues know that if they bring enlightenment to someone, that person will become a more useful member of society and will help other people, and that end goal is what they care about, not short-term social agreement. They may care about fitting in or gaining approval, and they may need to hide the truth of what they really think to survive at work, but if it leads to not teaching other people what they know, then they are in a trap. You see, even if you don't think a blue should have said what they said, if they said it, consider the source. Blues talk without filters sometimes, because they're channels of the divine. That thing they said might be your message from God, even if you don't want to hear it.

### Breaking Through the Mental Gridlock

If you've ever suffered from not being able to change your mind, consider a blue's job. Sometimes, they have to take a jackhammer to your ignorance. That's another reason they say things so boldly and speak in opposites. It's one of the ways they can get you to let in their light. Somehow, a blue must slip around your preconceived notions and soften your cherished thirty-year truths. Sometimes, they have to crack that egg. So, feeling internally that there is truth on both sides of a polarity, for different reasons, reminds you that it's your attachments, close-mindedness, and stubbornness that often holds you back. Often what is necessary to break these things is the reality that nothing stands alone. Everything is connected; one action relates to another, one idea is both it's up and it's down. If you can step on both sides of the fence, you can invite people to the other side for their own good so they are inspired to change for the better. Hence, a working out of the teacher's will is to preclude the suffering of another with the proper knowledge, preparation, and know-how. Speaking in opposites, saying things like "living in the country is best, but you have to live in town" helps people release their fears and come to consensus. Once you see both sides of the same coin, you feel you can succeed at the task at hand. It is a blue's way of helping you see something new.

For themselves, blues know that to bring themselves back into balance, they must sometimes even live at the opposite end of the spectrum from where they used to be. They must try out thoughts that oppose the old positions they used to take. If they don't, they can't learn about the whole, and they can't relate to all people.

### Time is Fluid

A blue's concept of time will get them into trouble, though it is a gift, not a trap. Blues don't follow other people's clocks, they follow their own, and that's because they are working to follow the flow of what is happening and often need to complete an experience before they can teach it. While a blue can train themselves to be punctual, having a natural sense of time based on the connectedness of the universe and following divine timing instead of human timing is how they prefer to operate. They let things happen outside a linear flow, according to the needs of the whole universe, not just your bosses'. It's part of what makes blues be on purpose. And they are a dominant spiritual gift; they like to lead the way.

### Communication Style: General vs. Specific

The blue communication style is general, not just specific. Blues don't need to focus only on specifics—they use specifics when imparting what they know, especially when it comes to teaching you how to apply knowledge. Sometimes, the details are necessary to communicate, or a subject will be misunderstood. What makes blues stand out is how they are willing to make broad, generalized statements about how to proceed. They have to talk to all of the spiritual gifts, and all people—so they must use general language that appeals to the universal. Also, since blues must check in with their emotions on a regular basis if they want to stay in their gifts, and also speak from spirit, they lean toward giving you principles and guidelines to follow that they feel will help you avoid possible pitfalls that may come up. They can empathize with you as an individual, but they can also see how your pain or your problems are reflected in countless others. (For them, each person is connected.) They care so much that you come to know what they know because it helps everyone when you change. You will create a ripple effect. It's that stone in the water that blues are always throwing. They are experts at finding the right stone to toss to create the biggest and best ripple effect.

Blues help you, but they also help humanity as a whole with each thing they say. For blues, all people are one, and that's something they constantly feel and know whenever they talk to just one member. It's this connection to all people that gives them the ability to generalize. Some people confuse a blue teaching about a group of people as their stereotyping, but blues make general statements about everything under the sun. For a blue, groups and individuals are interchangeable. You are one with all of humanity, and you deserve the advice and the content that all of humanity has to provide.

### Negative Experiences Are Nice

Blues love to experience life, and they love to see how a teaching plays out in the real world. They appreciate how life isn't always a bed of roses and value the negative for its ability to train you into being a better human being. Since the most important thing is education, the learning that results from experiences can actually justify them and make them worthwhile. It's the balm that cleans the divine mind, the comfort that even an unfortunate circumstance can be what was best for you at the time. Blues tend to see the inherent value in all experiences, though they will still help you see possible consequences for actions, since that is one of their best fortes to help with right-action.

### Equality Comes First

Blues like to treat everyone equally. They don't see why one person should be seen as more important than another. No matter how much status or how many accolades a person receives, a blue will still think of that person as an accessible person. A person with dignity, but a person with human failings, all the same. Though anger can be a deadly trap for them, nothing makes blues angry like perceived inequality, and its inequality they perceive ahead of almost anything else sometimes, when they walk into a room. Listen to blues talk and you'll hear about the unfairness in the world. They don't necessarily complain about it, but they do notice it and they do point it out. Life isn't fair, and it can be difficult for a blue to understand that. It is something they attempt to rectify. When they can't succeed is when they can feel out of control and can end up resorting to violence, like Jesus in the temple.

Blues are preoccupied with what the Buddhists call "right-action." Community-minded, they want people to do right by each other, and they would never agree with someone who would say that someone else doesn't have value because of placement on the hierarchy. Blues really do get caught up in wanting to be the student and also the teacher, the cop and a member of the gang, the artist, and the spectator. Opposites attract because they are two parts to a whole, and if they don't perceive the wisdom of both sides, they can't say anything profound. Now all of this is good for students, because blues do treat their students, when they teach in an actual classroom, equally. No student is better or worse than another. Blues do not discriminate when it comes to who needs to learn from them.

## Presentations of Fact

If you have a natural teacher in your life, he or she will figure out the information that you know, how it relates to what they know, and will present both as fact. They will spontaneously introduce, inform, connect, and conclude for an individual or a group when needed and when necessary. This is what allows them to be called "teacher"; this is the behavior that we say "enlightens." Natural teachers must talk a lot, not simply to inform you but to inspire you to do and be better (the goal of all their work) and thus aim to make the world a better place. Now, better is a point of view. However, blues think that when you account for certain important things—which could be values, facts, consequences, or wisdom—you will love your life more. The teaching blues do is about everyone, bringing people together, and helping them to choose more wisely to make their own lives more fulfilling, happier, and the world a more equal and equitable place—a place where love and wisdom have big roles.

## Blue Traps

### Anger

Anger results from not understanding why people do the things they do, why someone would neglect to account for possible consequences of their actions before taking a step. Blues are so good at connecting action and consequence, it becomes their

Achilles' heel. If any kind of self-absorption has taken hold, they can become tricked into thinking that all people have this famous ability, when in fact, they do not. When we are in our traps, we forget that other people do not possess the gift we do. This holds true for all colors. However, we were all sent to do our gift. It's mundane sometimes. Sometimes we don't want to get off the couch and give our gift to others. When people don't understand something, that is when blues need to teach them, not chuck them in the stupid box. When we are slowed down, when we are not in fight or flight, when we bring love to what we do, blues remember to teach instead of resist.

Blues can have a hard time accepting it if they tell someone something and that person doesn't apply the information. It's overconfidence. They think their knowledge is the end goal. They care about someone, but realize they must live their own life. Blues do not usually care what someone does with a particular piece of knowledge. That part is not that important to them in an enlightened state. When they are deeply involved with someone, and have a vested interest in a cause or a person, they do tend to be more attached to their words being heard. They can and should value their own knowledge. Sometimes they get used to people following them. Knowing so much more than some people about some things (or thinking they do) leads people to put them on a pedestal in terms of their knowledge and ability. As humans, we do become attached to what someone does with our knowledge and advice. This is an ego function, and it can trigger emotions and conditioning in a blue that results in their anger. Thinking people are stupid and judging their choices are results of being attached to points of view.

Since they are focused on what it takes for people in general to expand, cultural situations of unkindness and inequality in addition to people's personal problems can make blues frustrated because there is so much to do, love into being, and work on. Sometimes blues just don't want to do the work it takes to teach to the book (get people on the same page) and say what needs to be said. They wonder why others didn't come before them and make a difference already. It is easier to get angry and ask why certain people didn't prevent untoward things from happening in the first place. It is always easier to blame others than to take responsibility. When a blue finally gets fired up about what has not been done by an individual or a community of people, and then finally realizes they have to do something, attempting to fix the whole situation founded on ignorance in one fell swoop can create a big mess that involves numbers of people, scenes, and accusations. Blues may intentionally irritate, anger, or provoke others so that they have to pay for their ignorance.

### Drama

Drama is another key blue trap important for understanding this spiritual gift. There are two forms of the drama queen; when a blue does and doesn't cause drama on purpose. One can lead to another, and there is a continuum between the two. First, a lot of dramas start with someone becoming resentful that someone else didn't do things they "should" have done.

Blues can think that is the worst thing in the world. In their speech, manner, and tone, they can verbally dramatize the wrongdoing, making it bigger than it was. In essence, they make a mountain out of a molehill, and tell a story about what really happened that is disempowering. When blues start making decisions based on their stories, such as about how someone did something on purpose to cause harm, they can end relationships and refuse to talk to people. They take all their toys out of the sandbox and go home. Furthering a drama that was created between two people consists of fueling both sides of a conflict, which blues will do if they are really mad and can't see how to obtain justice.

### Not Teaching

Like all of the spiritual gifts discussed in this book, when a master chakra gift isn't being done by its carrier, that person is in a trap. Now, you don't have to do your gift 24/7, but that gift needs to be used in places where it's needed, called for, and can make a difference. That's answering the call to spirit.

### Knowing Everything

Finally, blues can make subconscious deductions, based on others' behavior and words, that they will never know as much as the blue does. This leads to aloofness and even snobbery. Others do have intelligence and are able to make it in life. Sometimes blues forget that in one way or another.

## All Apologies

Not everyone is good at apologizing. If this is something you want to be better at, focus on your throat chakra. Blues are good at apologizing, because like a pendulum, they will eventually swing to the opposite end from where they started. This liberates them, and it's inexorable. It can also liberate you. Like all people, blues can get stuck in their position. But then the universe usually provides them with a way to see the other side of the issue. The universe has a penchant for putting blues in their place— who can't help but see it when they wake up in the morning. Eventually they get there and see how their words play out with others, how they caused a person to feel bad or not do something. When blues fail to see the negative consequences that will befall them ahead of time, their nature allows them to understand life in reverse, to grasp reasons why things did happen as they did. Once a blue has experienced enough consequence as a result of their choices, it will make them apologize.

## In Sincerity

Natural teachers bring groups together or find groups where they can teach not only the content they are contracted to deliver, or choose to deliver, but share about themselves and sometimes, by example, their whole life to show you that there is a different way, a new way to be. They make connections for you to show you how you can improve, and they push you to improve. They are constantly expanding so you may expand. The knowledge they give you, they give you so you can move forward and choose from a more informed, liberating point of view—that's the whole purpose of wisdom, after all. It's something that needs to be actualized to be of any use. This is why they care about being heard and love to hear that their advice has been followed or taken into account (in your own chosen way). Yes, teachers know that there is another way to do things—always another way—because there is always a new perspective and a new breadth of knowledge to work in. They know this knowledge to be power, and so do you.

Teachers care that they are able to tell you what they know, and how to use it, so that you can be affected by that in whatever way you are meant to be. They trust you will use the knowledge and wisdom they provide you with to change your life, in whatever way you will do so, on your personal timeline. They have complete trust that once their thoughts have been spoken aloud to you, you will take it and run with it—at some point.

## Famous People with a Blue Master Chakra

Famous blues include Booker T. Washington, educator of slaves and former slaves, Martin Luther King Jr., an activist who preached equality, and President Barack Obama, who was the first person to make health care accessible to everyone in the United States. Mahatma Gandhi, who stood for the cause of justice and respected (treated as equals) all human beings is another blue. Gwyneth Paltrow, businesswoman, is aware that her life teaches others.

7

# PURPLES: THE
# NATURAL ARTISTS

What a purple does is love you as God loves you: nonjudg-
mentally, accepting you for who and what you are, most of the
time. They find ways to express themselves in all ways, shapes,
and forms to model authenticity and emotional availability in
kind, loving relationships. They love a variety of people, valuing
uniqueness and the differences found in people out of trust.
They also have the compassion and the strong conviction that
they can safely build a bridge to you so you can seek them out,
and vice versa. They manifest emotional freedom, trust, and
openness in their relationships because they want to work
together with people. They are able to relate to strangers as

though they were family members. Purples know what love is. Their interpretation of that focus is found in their voice, their eyes, their heart, and their look. When Jesus incarnated as a human being, he chose the purple soul-ray to guide him on his journey. As Christians often believe, Jesus was a man, and apart from how he has been used as an example to coerce others into following a specific spiritual path, he focused on being a teacher who brought enlightenment to humanity and taught love through his nonjudgmental and insightful stories about human experience. Therefore some people will comprehend what purples are like by looking at their own prior relationship with Jesus (if it happens to be a good one), and others will start to understand the historical figure for the first time by looking at their friends who master the purple soul-ray to see what he must have been like.

All purples are comfortable with a wide range of emotion—it's one of the signature features of their gift. Thus, like Jesus, they can be there for someone when things are not going well. In the midst of struggle, they love to love the person in dire straits. They love people with devotion, care about them and who they really are, and give the gift of their presence and time to assist those people who have been less fortunate and need their love.

## Defining an Artist

The term "natural artist" refers to a person who wants to create emotionally evocative and emotionally inspirational art. Our intentions affect the product when we're producing something.

Motivation is key. People with this master chakra intend, when they perform, to inspire people to learn how to be whole emotionally. They don't go about creating their art because they want to satisfy an internal desire to express themselves alone, regardless of its effect on others. That's not how they operate. Purples want their art to be beautiful, even as it considers the shadow side of humanity. Natural artists find canvasses everywhere, and when they intend to create art, they use both traditional and nontraditional forms. For example, some hairdressers and food-service workers may not consider themselves artists, but the way that they do their work shows they are finding a way to share a love lesson. Design is important to them in all they do—in the way they look, dress, and love. Love has a broad definition, but here it means actions that encompass the effect of raising someone to their next level, emotionally and physically. The act of raising someone's overall energy level and quality, even if that process is not always expected, allows someone to feel good about themselves. A natural artist looks at the world as a space in which love can be built, and then asks, "How do I accomplish that?" Their art explores that question.

## Purple Gifts

### Artistic Ability

Purples have to create anything from high-end paintings to rustic art. You can't put it into a box in terms of how it looks. Yet each piece is dynamic, multi-layered, and strives to bring people together in a specific way. Reality has many doorways, and they want to create one where peace and harmony reigns. It sounds idealistic, but it's their path. The third eye, where we imagine who we are, has rods and cones in it, and visions come unbidden through this energy center. Part of living on the purple soul-ray means you gain access to an overabundance of warm, loving energy that goes out to others in addition to an always fiery passion that burns inside. The purple energetic focus is forced to express itself in terms of what it sees, because it originates through the third eye into the tertiary human experience. Since chaos is always available as a formula for inspiration, it can be manifested most easily. Purples want to create a vision, because if they don't, the chaos will take over. The organized pictures are more real than the other ones, and they become the movie we watch when the purple turns on their film reel; those pictures will become part of our lifestyle whenever we hang out with them.

## Analysis and Holographics

When they create, purples evaluate with the mind who they are and what they want to do. They strive to purpose their art for what needs clarification in people's lives to help connect humanity, person to person. They not only use their right brain to gain a vision of what to create, they use their left brain to think through how they could best express their inspiration. For this reason, purples will analyze while they do what they do and wherever they go. They know how something should be made (as in construction), executed (as in dance), and expressed (as in theater). Singing and dancing is their natural area of talent, but so is any kinesthetically driven art form. They intuitively understand how to move gracefully in a flow. Their solar plexus chakra helps them here. They can use this to their advantage when they perform in a theater or when their job demands safety, as in construction. If they need to learn a different craft to express their visions than they already know, they will do it as soon as they can. Usually they will seek technical skill to complement their chosen field where they build their structure of creation.

Beauty is in the eye of the beholder, and when purples look at the world, they see emotion attached to each person, place, and thing. They imagine how a canvas might be worked with to structure various emotional elements for the purposes of coming to a conclusion; beauty is the standard by which they measure whether that conclusion is true or not. This is how truth and beauty got to be linked and why purples like yellows. As John Keats once said, "Beauty is truth, truth beauty." But instead of verifying facts, purples hone in on what they do and don't like in terms of shape, color, and form, to find the truth. Their brain is little involved—well, the right brain is, and the left brain less so. That's how they come to be able to paint when untaught. They are holographic in their mind's wanderings, wanting to express feelings and a quality of effervescence when they structure art.

## The Result

Performing art, of all kinds, is their way of helping us grow. This kind of musing comes naturally to a purple; their visions and becoming interested in expressing them is focused on growing, changing, and expanding. They picture what they want to see in the world. Chaos contains the elements of creation and thus, even garbage is a vision of beauty. The natural artist brings into harmony what doesn't look or feel right. It's the energy of love that a purple brings into their art when they are in their gifts that makes a way for us to walk inside it. It's how they attain depth on the two-dimensional plane. Love is in the air; they reveal that. Art is important to life. It's the focus and the medium through which we can remember who we really are and stay focused on that. In general, purples aim to create something that uplifts people or helps people release emotions, rather than putting up with insipid environments, clothing, and relationships that seem too focused on stasis. They will search for who they want and what they need rather than compromising on source materials.

## Hands-on Labor

Purples do not have an aversion to working with their hands. They wade knee-deep into hands-on work and cause respect to increase for those who do such work. Even if it is a desk job, purples have a way of diving into the process of creation that seems very hands-on. They are down-to-earth and comfortable with themselves, because in order for them to do their best, they must think about their work deeply and sincerely. They must get real with it and come into contact with it. Only when they don't handle issues with kid gloves do they actually produce their best work. The time and effort they put in satisfies and feeds them. It's the way they work and what they put into it that equals love. It's the transmutation of the many emotions, the experience their art creates, that attracts people to it. It's good that purples are willing to spend the time, effort, money, and loving attention on their creations. They need to be committed to holding their vision in order to have enough energy to make it real. Time spent between projects is an incubation period that actually increases the quality of the next artistic creation they'll bring into being. It is not important that purples make all of the creations they can come up with; there isn't time for everything.

## Discernment

When a purple sees visions about how something is supposed to be, or what they are supposed to make, it places them in a position of intolerance toward anything less. They become impelled to gratify their desire for what they saw in their head (always better than what they see out in the world) by creating that item. Finished creations are either "awesome" or not. They either really like something or they really don't. They also have strong emotions, both positive and negative, about how to do things socially. They talk to people through their art and engage them in what they want them to do. They want to be the ones to manifest the appearance, not to mention content, of the object or relationship. This is how they take control in the marketing field. They are confident in what they know about art. They will often point out what doesn't match or is disproportionate in another's appearance, or in the appearance of anything they own. They are good at pointing out flat, unemotional, unmoving art, music, and appearances—even the stuff everyone else likes. They should criticize other people's aesthetics, and if they don't, they're suppressed in their gifts. They see outside the boundaries of other people's, especially other color's visions, and tastes. They seek a new creation that brings love into the fold, so they need to name it.

## Spiritual Teaching

Design, where form meets function, creates order and harmony in both our physical and psychic environment, allowing people to connect to the real truth of who we are. A purple's goal as an artist is to guide us home through their point of view. That's how they get to become spiritual teachers in addition to artists. Purples enrich time with the things they make from what they see, and they always are sacred cows for that person. Any master chakra ultimately finds it's area of dominance to be important—that's how their ability to decorate anything helps the world to live less embargoed with baggage to weigh it down, lighting up the world with beauty and presence. It's a trap if they fail to. If purples don't create something that enriches people's experience on this planet, its appearance will reveal it. Their love will fail. In their gifts, they work to give to the world what it needs to return humanity to its own loving, kind nature. Isn't that what Jesus discussed and taught? They see into your soul with their powerful, love-streaming third eye. That's how he found his insights. Jesus was a really cool lightworker who was psychic. Purples use their psychic awareness to understand other dimensions and bring them here, connecting us with the love of the entire universe.

## Marketing

Our purples today come from the same place internally. Once, two of them gave me the exact same critique of a wedding invitation. One was a man from Iraq and the other was an American woman. This is possible because when an art form is going to be shared as a way to get people involved in an experience, the people of this soul-ray often know that certain relationships among style and form must be honored. They are good marketers because they look underneath the emotions to see what creates them, follow that back to the beginning, and decide what lines, colors, and shades will give them the reaction they are looking for. Advertising and marketing connect people to worthwhile activities that can only be experienced if someone is emotionally moved (otherwise they might not be inspired) to get out of their chair, pick up the phone, or buy something.

## Interpersonal Awareness

Purples strive to stay in control of the human interactions taking place around them. They use their psychic powers to make things less choppy and then knit together seemingly unrelated aspects of different people to smooth out relationships. They aim to make the complex more basic when it comes to feelings. They can explain the interpersonal on both an intuitive level and from the perspective of raw knowledge. This is how people sometimes experience their knowledge being shared—as raw. Their ability to see other people's motives and intuit what they'll do is based on their willingness to look at the dark and light sides of people. They tend to be realistic about humanity and what we do, because they know people. They consider how they know people to be a point of praise. As reality experts in human dynamics, they sharpen their skills by bringing love to the table when it isn't being served. They open their hearts and talk to people, getting their attention, teaching them how to want more and still get what they need. Purples want the best for people.

## Aiming for Victory

It's just natural for people with a master purple chakra to aim high. If you're going to have a relationship, why have a bad one? It needs to feel a certain way and be of high quality. If you're going to bother planting a garden, it needs to be weeded so that it looks pretty. Victory is a quality in their blood. They move toward it, even in their sleep. But in spite of their focus on having the best and being the best, any purple can surprise you with their mix of luxury and down-to-earth humility.

## Al

Like many purples, Al had an inscrutable set of realities. His favorite experience in all his life was the time he went to the Louvre in Paris. The son of millionaires, he wanted to be poor. He liked to dress old. Both his viewpoints (he felt the world was going to be worse, not better) and the way he made his living passed for working class. He did assembly in a local factory-like setting. One evening as I was hanging out with the web-designing crew, Al called. We talked for a while. When I got off the phone, I mentioned that he was bummed because he didn't have a car, and that he had just sold his BMW. My friends who were living in a dumpy house, laughed. They expected him to be a typical guy: either rich or poor—not a rich person who was poor. He was fascinated by constructing his own life according to his own choices. He liked wondering how to do things in new ways and being someone who stood out. He lived in a mansion on a trust-fund pittance, his version of the starving artist, and wanted to move west away from Chicago. His art form? Making guns. In his free time, he could tell a story that made you feel like you were in it. He picked up on all the emotional nuances in a determined way and called you on your emotions before you even had a chance to reflect on what they were. It was another one of his callings.

Al was one of my single friends who was looking for love. Like many purples, he kept his primary romantic relationship for a long time, over a decade, which for someone in his early thirties was all of his adult life. But Al had lost his wife for reasons even he couldn't say. Like the purple spiritual gift, Al was able to recall the great romance of his past in vivid detail and claimed his power through it, saying that to be in a relationship was his destiny. He remembered the time he took his woman canoeing and how she loved it. I was struck by the heart of gold in his willingness to bring such experiences to another person he didn't yet know. It was clear he did not want a relationship for his sake alone. Al would wear his baseball cap low and grouse about how everyone had a tattoo. He condescended to be my friend because I had no tattoos and did cartwheels in the parking lot upon request. (Purples like it when you perform.)

Finally, one day, after critiquing everyone else's body art, he sat up straight and said, "Hey, I think you should get a tattoo of two tuning forks, crossed, on your neck." That was Al for you—purple to the core. After all the time he spent criticizing other people's taste in art, the Universe kicked him into the flow. They are in touch with the energy of the Universe through which we all create. It's a beautiful energy that feels like a fountain. They can connect you more than other colors. In the end, it was experience that mattered—what he felt with anyone around him. He saw that a tattoo could express someone's path—that I had joined a tribe, that I should express it. Purples encourage you to be who you are with no reservations.

Speaking of which, Al couldn't stop talking about finding the right person, but he didn't seem needy—he was determined. The fact that his last relationship had lasted as long as it did was really important to him. Yet he was not stopping there.

While most people might say they want to be in a good relationship that knows no bounds, purples are the hardest workers. Al called any of his dates a "meeting" because it was work to him. He told me that he was open to finding anyone, as long as it was the right person—but that the right person could be someone he found under a bridge. That person he would find, he implied, wouldn't have to fit standards, as long as he could love them. Like many of my purple friends, Al spoke dreams into reality. Years after becoming Al's friend I met an artist who I had a strong connection to on the sidewalk in a foreign country after walking out from under a bridge. A unique mix of high and low—exacting, but at the end of the day, relenting—purples find ways to create and defy imagination. It isn't a myth. It's a reality. Their reality.

### Ability to Act on and off-Stage

Purples love to become the person you need them to be in order to love you. Sometimes they lose themselves in playing their many roles because they love to merge with the other person's needs and play to them. It's part of the creation process. They will change themselves around different people because they are great at acting and enjoy pleasing the crowd. This is how they are able to be the best actors and actresses. Manifesting a new personality, complete with new motives and all the trappings, can do more harm than good at times. Regardless, that's how the neighbor who yelled at you one day for not mowing your lawn effortlessly becomes the stand-up guy living the American Dream the next moment, while telling everyone he never bothered you. Purples can use emotions to change reality, for better or worse.

## Manifestation Ability

The purple master chakra has an amazing ability to manifest that which they desire. Their imagination is strong, powerful, and as a group, they are psychic. Creation comes as second nature to them. With their energy dominant at the third eye chakra, they picture what they want to have happen in their lives as a matter of course. Since they are so focused on feelings, and look for love among them, purples get to know themselves along the lines of what they do and don't want. They can differentiate what they do from what they don't wish to have around. To manifest any desire, one must really, really want it. Well, purples are the most passionate people! They have no trouble coming up with not only a desire but a deep desire for what they want. All emotions are their bailiwick, and all are honorable. Purples receive the messages inside the feelings and act accordingly. Therefore they can become very rich because they have the ability to vibrate, and conjure up feelings-wise what they want, and stay away from what they don't. Purples can also teach you what they know about how to manifest whatever you need.

## The Teaching of Love

Purples themselves teach love directly through speech, trying to get closer to your darkness, to transmute it. They help you shift your emotional state through their interactions. They are open to helping anyone. Even when you barely know them, they'll give their advice on how to handle your feelings and get on the same level with you in order to engage with you. They speak in profundities and mini-lessons. They are humanitarians at heart, and incorporate themselves in the world in so many ways to change it in order to bring more love to people. This is why they start businesses, write TV shows, and become science teachers. How to get along and relate to others, how to feel, and how to work together are basic topics they master, discuss, and teach in multitudinous ways.

Purples like to witness you being the divine for others, doing your best, laboring for that which you love. They can relate to love. They cannot abide for long the intolerance of the world that judges them and claims they are crazy, due to their emotional states…this is where the stereotype of the insane artist knocks on their door. They can't stand how they wanted something more—they wanted to create something for the world and needed emotional support for themselves to do it, but they got nothing for their trouble. They can be hurt by lack of love. They don't intend to take it out on you, but be aware of this.

## Purple Traps

### Not Good at Making Do

Status can be a stumbling block for purples who think they must have the best materials before they can focus on creating things to match their vision. When the perfect things they need don't show up as such on the topside world, they can withdraw and be snobby—not wanting to interact with the people around them or combine the best materials with the less-than-the-best to do what they need to do. But this is what life requires. It's important not to pressure them but instead express care and genuine kindness. But sometimes purples must know that in order to proceed, we must make do. Ironically, purples may need to lower their standard in order to stay in their gifts and keep going. By doing so, they restart the engine. The way to regain perspective after it's been lost is to receive the abundance they have access to.

### Speech Contains Feelings, Not Just Facts

They must process emotions all the time; they always think about how they feel. The things they say reflect their internal turmoil if bothered. For some purples, the things they decide to say don't necessarily express what they believe, but express feelings—and the two can get mixed up. Like anyone else, purples can wish to express emotions along with thoughts, but they use language as a tool of manifestation differently than other colors, because they are willing to speak the future to power. Their speech at any time then may not reflect positions they hold, but rather radical positions they want to hold. In short, when they talk, some purples always express their feelings (not facts) and sometimes also the future. Knowing this can help you remember not to rely on them to always mean what they say literally. Purples analyze, think, and feel. It all comes out. This can be a gift or a trap. It depends on the result.

## Pushing Buttons

Since it's pretty difficult to be in a relationship with purples without giving them access to your life, get ready to be emotionally vulnerable. In their gifts, they love to listen to your stories and help you get over them. They are just unable within their traps to be a directly loving and kind person all the time. They can manipulate people with emotional kindness by betraying their trust. It's nice to know that anytime a color goes into their trapped state, they're trying to do their gift, they just don't know how to. As Jesus would say, they don't really know what they're doing. Purples will try to get you to do what they want you to do unconsciously by hitting all the triggers they can find (which they find through intuition). Their tripping of our emotions sevenfold will cause us to have to stop and do a lot of sorting. Additionally, it will take us some time to learn the lessons they have to teach us through their button pushing.

Yet in their traps, purples will destroy what they decide they cannot love, whether that be a person's self-esteem or their plans. The opposite of love is fear. In protest to their lack of loving environment, they don't create, they destroy. It's basic instinct, located in the amygdala, the lower brain. With so many emotional connections hooked up between you and them (because their main chakra is emotional), they can very easily make you feel all of your immediate pain under the surface. When emotionally triggered, which often happens when they feel hurt, they may say harsh things that upset you on purpose. They can accomplish this through a few words, creating anywhere from a small to a large amount of fallout—it depends on the prior relationship. Purples are good at being love, and part of their loving you is helping you release that baggage. In this sense, they do you a favor when they hurt you.

Purples have their own baggage to unload, and no one is capable of loving all the time. They need our love and understanding; it helps them relate to us and love us back. Most of the time purples want to make you feel good—unless they're in their traps. Sometimes when they're in the trapped state of existence, in the throes of ego, they really won't understand how to love you over the long haul because they'll be busy using their emotions to go to next steps. They'll seek emotional experiences for the sake of feeling powerful, not because they lead to something good.

### Materialism and Lesser Products

If an artist profits from their work in order to sustain themselves, they can be fine, but by getting overly focused on making money and turning their work into a money-maker, purples must take care. When they stop focusing on the real reason they wanted to contribute in the first place, and lose conscious awareness of their inherent purpose, which is to give the world something it needs, the art suffers. How they create becomes "sold," and people can tell. The resulting products won't have the quality that attracted people to it in the first place. At some point, when quality is lost, the art won't move. It's when they are in their traps that purples create art that gives you cause to pause for the worse. Put another way, since love is who they are, they can lose themselves when they focus too much on money. One of the ways they stop themselves from falling into this trap is by charging a very reasonable price for what they create.

### Heart Contains Art

The purple spiritual gift teaches us how to love (what it means, why it's so important, how it's achieved, and how to open yourself up to it). They give love lessons verbally, through their perspectives and philosophies on life. They circle back to exploring love and how it works. Their words create a spiral, always circling back to what's really important. In their gifts, purples teach us how to create anything we desire to have or experience: they also teach us how to love anything. To wit, they make things for you to show you love.

## Famous People with a Purple Master Chakra

Famous purples include John Lennon, who was a visionary singer, and former Illinois Governor Rod Blagojevich. In his gifts, he gave children health insurance in Illinois. In his traps, he sold a senate seat. Quite a few actors and actresses are purple, such as Angelina Jolie and Johnny Depp.

8

# Violets: The Natural Helpers

Violets freely become any of the other colors in the master chakra system in order to do what needs to be done in the world around them. They fill in the gaps for everyone and are the only master chakra to become another very easily, whenever needed, and often. Becoming a chameleon takes up a major portion of their time and awareness. They blend the work of leader, promoter, thinker, fixer, teacher, or artist in with their own means of serving, which comes directly from the crown chakra wheelhouse to move everyone into the next stage of their being. Violets do what needs to be done no matter what, which is why they reach for the other chakras more than anyone else. Finally, when one of the other colors is missing, a violet will simply take their place. Violets put themselves last and others first. They are the ones who do this.

## A Basic Definition

Violets stand first among their friends to be described as extremely nice, empathetic people. The nicest of the nice, they receive the nickname "saint" from some of their friends. That's because no other color as consistently shares unconditional love in word and deed. They come across softly and gently; they speak with kindness and compassion. Each gift has special powers and abilities, and violets are no exception. These experts at people-service know what to give us before we know what we need. They address what we must do physically to maintain ourselves and our work by working with us, side by side. They give us comfort when we feel burdened or otherwise uncared for; they pitch in wherever they are needed for the care and refinement of earth's humanity, environment, and animals. They shine their light brightly so we can see it. We know them by the light in their eyes and in their work, and they are drawn to help us. They soothe and calm the fears. They listen. They channel the divine in certain ways so that we can hold and see the light; they make everything brighter when going about their work. They can't help it. You feel touched by an angel when you walk by a violet, man or woman.

The kinds of service-acts violets perform require their attention to details, so they pay attention to them. They want to have

everything they need to help you with your project. Their clos-
ets are stuffed with supplies that someone they might encounter
might need. Violets follow others' direction with close attention,
taking instructions in quickly and executing them efficiently. No
one wants to be called a follower, but following someone else's
lead is a valuable skill that has merit throughout our industrial
world. Violets come by following nature honestly. That means
they tune into a pile of different energies, findings, and sources in
order to help accomplish a goal for others. They work on people to
make them whole. They work on endeavors they can get behind
for the good of all. They can function alone and independently
or attached to a group. There, opportunities arise for them to
delegate all the things that need to be done for the rest of us. This
makes them lead-helpers.

### How Their Light Affects Them

Because their master chakra generates light at the top of the
chakra system, they are irrigated by its light and often receive
buckets of the highest frequency that can be received on any
soul ray. Crown chakra light saturates their mind, their heart,
their being. That's why they are constantly under the influence
of love and compassion and distribute it without thinking. They
are very sensitive to their surroundings, their feelings, and other
people and where those energies are. In addition, violets' access
to the entire spectrum of light, or all the master chakras, allows
them to connect energetically with a number of people in a number of ways that others would find overwhelming. They can even

be overlooked or go unnoticed because of the softness and inherent high vibration of their light. Their light being so flexible that they blend into a crowd unnoticed, they softly and easily assist, giving them precedence. Their light facilitates this.

### How They Embody the Crown Chakra

People can experience unconditional love from a violet who is in their gifted state. Their focus on serving others allows this to be so. It comes from their ability to see the divine plan through their divine connection to God, which they do and the rest of us can't understand. It makes it easy for them to channel compassion and goodwill in situations others resist and even hate. Though they can do much to discredit themselves, their vibrational frequency will always call them back to a point of creating from spirit what needs to be done in the physical.

Violets use the energies, or gifts of the other chakras, from the inside out when doing their work. They seem to have a special ability to take ownership of another spiritual gift and use it from its own vantage point. Because they aim to use it specifically to help another person, they get to know it very well. This is why violets are referred to as a jack-of-all-trades. They go visiting. When they visit another chakra, they blend with its energy in order to become that gift. The reason for this is because they are specifically focused on helping another person whenever they do what they do. No other master chakra focuses on helping per se—they focus on helping through doing something else, like fixing something or teaching something. Violets use the other gifts in order to help.

## Violet Gifts

*Regarding You As Your Best Self*

The last thing a violet would do is get in your way, creating an obstacle, emotional or otherwise, that impedes you. If you betray a violet, he or she can still speak to your good qualities. They can still think of you as your greatest self, not your B-grade one. They wish to interact with you even when you can't live up to their standards. This can sometimes cause a lot of pain in the person who must hear how great they are when they are misbehaving. When he was five years old, my ex-husband said something to his mother that caused her to slap him. Right after that, he said, "Do you feel better about yourself now that you've done that?" After this incident, she didn't want to be alone with her son for the rest of the day. It was because he had held a mirror to her and asked her if it matched her best self. Violets with less self-control can't do this as effectively, but it's within every violet's power to hold the divine version of you up for you to see—with or without strategy. I have seen some violets surprise and distress their friends by talking about the important things either they themselves or the other people were going to do in the future. Most of the time these were positive visions, but when someone tells you that you can be the principal of your school, and you are just a teacher, it can cause anxiety or fear of success. Have you ever felt unworthy of what a violet told you you could become?

## Connecting to Others

Violets have a lot of feelers out there gently touching the people that they help. That's the way they learn how to time when to do things; they feel the subtle signals in the energy of others, in the energy grid, or web, that we're all a part of. Their own energy is often engaged far away from them through the ethers. You can tell this is so because when they do get grounded and release this energy, they get back such a large amount of their own energy in return that they look brighter and instantly healthy. Normally a certain amount of a violet's energy is always engaged for others.

I once went to Target looking for moving boxes. I was walking down the aisle. I looked up and saw a person in a red vest look up at me from over twenty feet away. As soon as he did this, I knew he was a violet. I could feel his energy feeling my intentions. He knew he was going to help me next and waited for me to come over to him. My intention was strong that day and easy to pick up as a broadcast signal by an ever-attuned violet person who is in service to all. I had set an intent to find moving boxes and find them fast. People were swarming around him because it was so busy, but their intentions weren't focused the way mine were. I started speaking before I even reached him. He started walking to the correct aisle before I stopped speaking. That's how responsive violet energy is to someone's needs.

## *Helping Through Acts of Kindness*

Violets represent the ultimate support person you can have, the person who performs continual action on your behalf to be in service to you and move you into your next level. They directly involve their head and take charge of things hands-on; they don't sit at the sidelines and do nothing. They walk your path right next to you and help you with everything down to the minutest detail. This is how they serve the divine. That's why they are so happy to help you, and while they do, they are, of course, kind. To violets, God is love, and they are here to share that love, as God would, with others. Remember, God doesn't just perform huge acts of significance for all to see, but small acts of kindness no one sees.

To violets, getting the mail for you and doing your dishes is a sacred duty because it helps you take a step on your path of spiritual advancement and outfitting. They work to help you meet specific goals while doing everything administrative at the same time. They've got your back while also moving you forward step-by-step.

They like working in a group too; greater numbers focus the violet's attention and gives them a larger container in which to engage all their helpful mindfulness. Violets use a lot of energy in different places, so focusing on one large task with lots of moving parts is perfect for them. Even in a group, though, their focus remains on the individual. How can I help this person, they ask? Through the people that they help, they support a cause with the investment of energy, time, and awareness. And the cause they must support becomes important to them over time whether they consciously choose it or not.

### Working Diligently—On Behalf of Others

Violets can be, but don't have to be, worker bees. They typically occupy themselves in whatever most basic or refined way suits them. For example, some nurses work in home care and some work in the emergency room. There are more and less complex ways to serve. All violets can be proud of what they do because for them, service is never secondary—it usually connects to what physically needs to happen for things to go well, and they are proud to support physical service tasks. Their goal is that things go smoothly. Therefore, violets perform jobs across the board. They are the best spiritual gift to employ as secretaries. But they don't all want to be secretaries. They could be the CEO of the company. If they do this, they will perform the job like a violet. Because cleaning the kitchen is so much more than it appears to be. Sometimes to clean up that world and get it arranged correctly means you just have to be the CEO instead. They bring their unending spiritual energy down to the physical world to open the doors so that others may go through. There are more violets in existence than any other color because they let the other master chakras do their jobs.

What sets violets apart from the other master chakras is the characteristic of taking any job from the standpoint of serving all. Violets do any job in order to serve the people involved. For example, one violet I know is a school superintendent.

However, when she talks about her mission, she indicates that it is to help the children. Now anyone could say that. However, she means it strongly. Her goal is to be in service first, rather than getting the district to a better bottom line. She might do that too, but if she does, it will be to create the best possible experience for the children in her district. Service comes first, with the thought being, "how may I help the people under my jurisdiction?"

With service being of primary importance, violets will do anything and can do anything as part of their mission to serve. Judging the fact that violets want to do the little things sometimes holds them back in understanding their own importance. Other people can refuse them for wanting to get them a glass of water. This is not love, but still: what other people find tedious, violets find essential because of the way in which they show care through the activity. When other people would rather do something more important or more interesting, there is usually a violet who will find it more than acceptable to do that job in style. It isn't what they do, it's how they do it that makes it violet. That's the way it is with all of the gifts—it's how we do what we do, and why, that determines our master chakra.

The reason violets won't mind doing something basic for someone, even if they catch themselves in a hierarchical system where the person has a lot of power, is because they believe that giving you their care, concern, attention, and kindness is enough. It is important. They understand that ultimately they do whatever they end up doing on an individual level for the greater good of all. They like to think globally, act locally. They are masters of that.

## *Raising Us Unconventionally*

Violets love to raise children because they like to teach people how to be in the world and work together without problems, in harmony. If there are no children around, violets are equally inclined to see adults as children—of God. Just getting things done is never enough for them. In their gifts, they work to teach us how to do what they do, how to be more compassionate, and nicer to others as we live our lives. They model it, they discuss it. They critique others' behavior. They give us pointers, if they can. What's that, you say? Functional behavior being taught reflexively by humans? Yes, it does happen. Most people don't teach other people how to be civil, affectionate, loving people, but violets do—or can, if they don't. That's what makes them unconventional. They seek out ways to teach tolerance and high standards of behavior. Still, they don't want to harm us or upset us in the process. They believe that our feelings matter and need to address our concerns one by one to get the job done right, locked up, if you will.

Whenever Anastasia and I would hang out, whether at my house or hers, she would help me with how I was doing. I remember once when she said, "you really need to work on your emotions, it's like a two out of ten." I didn't know exactly what she meant, but I also knew that she couldn't break the violet code of saying how bad it really was. So, I had to decide. In addition, she needed to put her statement so I would pay attention and not get offended by it. She wanted to push me gently into the pool, not throw me in. It was sweet, kind, and clever.

I also remember that she once defended me for being stressed out to one of our other friends by saying, "She faces rejection every day in her business." I never forgot that she said it. She could always see the information in the person who was being made wrong, so they would not be wrong. She could always illuminate what was going on. She was a lantern. Violets give insights to connect awareness so we will be at peace with what *is*. They prioritize what is being okay.

### Violets and Frugality

Violets seem to have a special ability to carve up a dollar in more ways than any other color because of the way they approach service. Even though violets can have enough money to spend freely, it bears mentioning that if they feel that money is tight, they will figure out how many people can best be served—or rather, how many purposes can be served by just ten dollars. They will leverage that energy as far as it can go, figuring that ten dollars can buy bus transportation for two to a park for a homemade picnic instead of being spent on a shirt. Life is better when we do it together, when we put our energy into another person.

### Lifting You Up

Violets are good at lifting people up by helping them feel good about themselves. When getting to know you, they become interested in who you are, in all the little details about you, and encourage you on your journey however possible. It can feel like flattery. One violet already mentioned here would say to certain people he knew, "you are a beautiful person." He not only believed what he said, they did. Violets share what they see, and they see a lot; their crown chakra position puts them in touch with the divine, and lets them unroll the divine plan like a map before battle. They can give us information about what is really going on from the master plan itself. You come to feel uplifted when they help you because they serve as the wind beneath your wings, not a viable force of power. They whisper, "it's time to go, it's time to grow."

They are gods and goddesses of love and compassion, like Kuan Yin. They want to give you what you want. It becomes easy to give someone a genuine compliment when you are always noticing details occurring to that person in their life, and can see their higher self at the same time. Violets are especially good at making connections between what happens and how people treat each other. They like to catch you being good and doing something right. They genuinely do this without being hard on others. In their gifts, they give criticism with mercy and kindness. Once, a violet coworker said to me, "You know, I don't think anyone around here really gets you! But I know when you walk out that door today you're not going to let that bother you." Was it criticism of the people who didn't get me, or of me for not teaching them how to get me? It's hard to tell. What mattered is she wanted me to know what she had observed. Violets help us to react less and become more responsive to whatever situations we encounter, because they want us to succeed. For them, success happens when we feel genuinely good about ourselves because we can handle what comes our way, and we don't need them anymore. They are like Mary Poppins. When they are needed, they land. When they are no longer needed, they fly away.

### Everything is Always, Already Okay: The Violet Philosophy of Living in This World

When in service, violets stay connected to the divine, exuding a sense that everything is ultimately alright. They personally know the contentment that lies within and behind things as a form of ultra-compassion. They transmit their sense of peace mixed with the love they help others with. It comes from an innate perspective that they have, that what they do is rightly arranged by the universe. They believe in the good in people. Since they know that more good exists than bad, that a plan is in place, and since they get in touch with how the vast universe is making sense on an energy level all the time, they roll with the punches. They have access to the divine perspective on what happens on earth from within their heart. This causes their heart to extend to all the world. If they do feel something is wrong, this is why they engage themselves to help. Their helping perspective arises from a higher perspective on belief in humanity and goals that bring us to a better place. Their sense of okayness succeeds even while helping people in a crisis because they don't think that anything is really unjust—ultimately, those situations are good for making things better. They wish to bring all that is into alignment with what is right, and due to humans in their evolved state. They take on acts of service because they believe people can be more than they have presently chosen to become. They can see these visions, these stars, from the crown chakra on top of the head, connected to the divine in ways no other color strives to be—in service to the divine, in service to all.

## Moving On, Giving Up

That being said, violets do not respect those who have a "never say die" attitude about life. If it's time to give up on the violin, it's time to give up. If you don't like it anymore or want it anymore, they can agree with you. Their gift is feminine, and like a feminine warrior goddess, they will end a creation when the time comes. When they feel that they have experienced enough with a certain person, or simply know they cannot continue to help them, that this person must help themselves, they will move on. If something isn't working out, they won't stay there indefinitely and wallow in the muck. They will also clean up their loose ends so that the person left behind doesn't have to worry about the fallout vibrations, financial and emotional, from the end of the relationship. At least they do their best to make this so. They have an innate sense of understanding that when they leave a person, it allows that one to move onto their next available opportunity. They have gotten that person as ready as they can for their new reality, and now it's time to let them fly and go and get it.

## Violets Go Last

Violets hold themselves back for others to take a place before them, mustering their ego for other times and places. They themselves put their own needs last. This is not necessarily a trap. They often do surrender to be last in something to serve the common good through allowing another to shine, to literally lift them into their greatness by holding space for them to become more of themselves. In these moments of letting someone else go first, they hold space for the divine to come in so that person can live in, walk in, and grasp his or her own capabilities. If you want to be more like a violet, then you must put your ego aside and be ready to channel the divine for others as you put their needs first. It's another aspect of bringing things to completion that violets see their place as "last." They see that that's exactly when it is their time to step in.

At the age of 95, my grandma once held my arm and had me sit with her while all of the other older people in the room got up to get their food at a party at her assisted living home. She sat there smiling and looking at all of the people as they stood in line. There was a light in her eyes and in her heart as she did. She was completely unconcerned about herself and didn't see herself as needing more than the others. In my mind, she deserved to be at the front of the line. But she was not in a hurry. The way she was helping her friends was to hold space for the divine to be there as she enjoyed them enjoying themselves. Whether such acts go unnoticed or not, they are crucial to allowing the light of love and compassion in the door. A practiced eye can spot more such acts of kindness.

## Violet Traps

Violets will use their own connection to love and compassion to gain the moral high ground. They will attempt to portray you as a less than kind person instead of negotiating for a solution to both sides in a conflict. That's because when they are on one side and you on another, and they go into a self-worth slump, it becomes hard for them to stay neutral, not judge, and see the positive on both sides, which is their gift, even when it comes to themselves. In their traps, they will tend to align with the person most in good standing with them, when that underdog, or even their over-dog, is wrong. They will rudely tell you that you suck because they have the better future. They usually actually say: "you are not being kind enough and you do not deserve X." This is a moral stance that comes from Christianity, which many violets have decided will be their motto when they are upset.

They can see truth, but not clearly enough when blinded by their own emotions in pain. They often get disabled by wanting to defend someone or something without thinking about the consequences. This comes from being too territorial without being grounded enough in reality. They will defend whoever they have decided needs saving unless shown a new way of being (even if that means themselves).

It's not the real reality they desire. It is the act of saving another, rescuing someone from their pain, which they value more because they are empathic. But they desire that which they feel will avert pain but doesn't actually do so. They simply choose their side, or choose who they are going to destroy today, and then try to smear your character.

Their desire to be good leads them to destroy the only relationship that could potentially bring them out of harm's way. They go on to choose the dungeon over being heard, the dungeon over stepping into the light, and the light of the garbage dump outside Jerusalem (Hell) instead of the porch light of someone who actually dares to defend them from danger. They will "be good" until it kills them. This is how they get walked on.

It is they who have the most to learn in such a case, because this kind of vindictiveness is a low form of one-upmanship, which comes from the amygdala, the survival brain. Violets are the least evolved when it comes to expecting other people to be like them (a trap of any color). Even though in their gifts they wear compassion like a glove, they can turn that hand and smack you across the face just as easily and smoothly as anyone when pained. So don't be fooled. A violet can hurt you just as much as any other color in their traps.

## Famous People with a Violet Master Chakra

Famous violets include Michelle Obama, who cares about everything, especially children, and Mother Teresa, who embodied compassion in her charity work. Another violet is Robert Herjavec from *Shark Tank*, because he always cares about the person behind the entrepreneur, wants to give them what they need, and is the least abrasive shark. Though not a pushover, he is generous with his money, often in contrast to his peers.

# 9

# SIDE CHAKRAS

In order to embody your spiritual gift, you have two chakras on either side of you to work with. If your gift is the sofa, they are your armchairs. You like to relax in them sometimes. You will tend to know the territory of these spiritual gifts better than any of the others. These chakras help you define and engage your gift in the world, be more flexible with it, and reach more people with more techniques. They are the colors you "shade" with. However, the more you develop as a person, the more insights into all of the chakras you'll receive, and the more you'll be able to use the functions of all the gifts, still retaining your dominant master chakra.

## How Do the Side Chakras Affect the Colors?

Reds need the orange on one side of them to be able to promote their ideas for their business and gain business contacts and colleagues. Having orange on one side keeps reds from getting too serious. They can be spontaneous instead of always grounding into their plan. Violet, on the other side of red, lets reds be gentle with others when needed and bring compassion to their leadership; it reminds them not to get overbearing in their leadership style.

Oranges can use their red side to stay focused and grounded, which is something orange by itself has trouble doing. Oranges use the research abilities and truth-seeking skills of the yellow chakra on their right to help them set up their lives and make decisions. Having red and yellow on either side of orange provides orange with enough analysis to be independent but the strength to remain in the flow of action. They work as stabilizing forces for orange, and in addition, let them "see" the fun that is coming up in the future. Yellow gives information about the big picture (red) that orange wants to enjoy!

Yellows have a tendency to stay in their heads, but their orange side reminds them to be social and lets them interact with others in a smooth and rewarding way. They become eager to share their information. Green on the other side allows them to actually go and fix some of the problems they work all day solving.

Greens need yellow in order to see what needs to be fixed in the first place. The yellow gift helps them be more observant, since yellows are the strongest at noticing details in the environment. Being able to see the "pathways" of truth also gives greens a reason to proceed with their healing and mending work. It allows them to test a solution they have in mind to see if it is right. Blue gives greens wisdom for what to do with the mystical knowledge they receive from the divine, which helps them apply practical solutions. Yellow keeps them balanced in the truth of these solutions, for any "fix" must be strong and well-founded in order to count for a green.

Blues benefit from being able to organize their knowledge, which green on one side gives them the choice of doing. Purple on the other side brings grace and creativity to their teachings and lets them pull love into them, too. It reminds blue that we are really all about love, and that is why we proceed. It lets blue be less mental and makes it easier to stay balanced in all four corners of mind, spirit, body, and emotion. Green contributes to this because greens are the most balanced, so it helps blue stay in touch with peace and the actual physical center of the body.

Purples need to be able to step back and go to a neutral place, to return to center. The emotional world and the chaos they can see and sometimes adore, and the tornado they are, craves a space of wisdom. They can use their throat chakra to get a different, more mental perspective on things and see what is "right" for them. On the other side, violet lets purples' love be characterized by compassion, not just romance. Because purples can be unstructured and even unstable, having blue on one side helps balance them, which can even encourage them into contemplation and authenticity, whereas violet on the other side keeps them connected to people and things at the same time, which helps purple stay current with events.

Violets are the only color that can shade to any color of the rainbow. However, violets do have two armchair colors, like everyone else. And on one side is red. Going to red lets violets be able to make decisions about what is best for all. It is the decisiveness that lets them move into action. Purple helps violets be creative in their solutions and service to others. This is important, because violets who cannot feel depth of emotion and have creative artistry in their work stand in danger of not feeling that it is worthwhile.

# 10

# Light Partners

Some of the chakras work especially well together because they have an affinity for each other's goals. This is a built-in compatibility of two or more colors. In general, you will usually have an affinity, or shared understanding, with those of your same chakra color. First, we'll take a look at light partners who are different colors, then we'll talk about how you can optimally work with your own color.

## Affinity Light Partners

Reds can easily partner with violets because violets are so good at serving a common goal. They enjoy and appreciate someone who can give them a foundation and provide for them so that they can carry out their true purpose. Reds desire to direct a common goal—they want to serve the community. They can form their own group with an individual violet. They can help violets manifest all sorts of different ways they can serve, and since reds are good at knowing what they want (they want to be in charge of setting the terms for what will happen, as chiefs), violets are their best team players, organizing, teaching, and nurturing the rest of the team that grows up around them, or within their nest.

Oranges blend very well with yellows, blues, and purples. Why yellow? Oranges find that their next steps lie in the off-beat wonderland that yellows are always exploring. In addition, because yellows can shade orange and oranges can shade yellow, they have long been working with the other's territory to accomplish their own goals, so they know it a little better than most. No one else meets at the intersection of orange and yellow except orange and yellow, after all. By using information to promote other people, places, and things, oranges obtain information. By accessing orange, yellows get in touch with being social like oranges do. So, they can be each other for each other. Orange needs yellow—otherwise it would just be an airhead. Yellow needs orange to communicate. Otherwise it will just be a strange, anti-social organism.

As for oranges and blues, oranges find blues give them a way back to themselves. Blues teach oranges about themselves, and vice versa. Like blues, oranges point out what can be learned from negative experiences. Oranges help blues rise to the occasion. Blues help oranges realize there is a limit to their happy dance and help them deal with the effects of negativity that has gotten them down in a constructive way.

Oranges and purples are the two master chakras that are "emotional," or their gifts are based out of emotion. As such, each really gets the importance of emotion and flowing with it. These two colors are able to communicate in emotionally provocative ways without scaring each other. They don't need words to communicate at all, however. The flow of emotion is enough to connect hearts.

Greens and yellows are able to concentrate on the same plane of specificity and appreciate the details required to do their work. Greens tend to be patient with yellows more than other colors, being able to follow their thought processes and gently help them work through problems and solve them. They grant yellows a loving kindness, helping them process their emotions and making it okay for them to be who they are. Greens inspire yellows to complete their tasks and projects by helping them work through the jungle of tasks that a yellow faces when they are trying to come to terms with the truth about a matter. Yellows help greens be of better service to the world by enlarging their ability to play in the world.

Blues find wisdom in the way in which oranges feel freedom, and blues give freedom when they teach. Blues also have an affinity for green. Healing is the natural result of much of teaching; growth and expansion is the result of healing, so these two are like yin and yang for each other, since greens trust blue's knowledge.

Purples love anyone who can form light from emotion, so oranges are good friends indeed. They just understand how each other operates. Purples love to play, and oranges are the masters of play. Purples, in that they accept all emotions, can help oranges process emotions when they are down, and oranges, in turn, like to keep purples happy, ensuring that the darkness doesn't take over the artist.

Violets have an innate ability to work with every color of the rainbow, but other than working well with themselves, they technically work best with reds. This is because serving others involves so many different kinds of activities—and reds can put boundaries around and focus on what the violet is going to work on.

## Same Chakra Friends

In general, when you work with people of your same master chakra, you'll get each other and accept each other's help more quickly, as long as there aren't personality conflicts. Reds will find it easy to work with reds, as both appreciate the fact that the other has objectives and is able to constitute present-moment action. Each understands the need for hierarchy and for that to be respected. Because they tend to appreciate traditional-style values, reds know where they stand with one another and can use their intuition in tandem.

Oranges have the most energy and insight into "play." So, other oranges keep up with them very well, and together they are able to keep the joy flowing at a high vibration. Expansion breeds expansion, after all. Oranges need other oranges to direct their energetic focus toward them so they can keep helping the other master chakras. It's hard to be the high point alone, without end.

Yellows appreciate each other's thought process. Both looking for data, each can provide the other with missing pieces. Because the primary way through to a yellow is through their intellect, other yellows can communicate very easily with them in expected ways. Yellows validate each other.

Greens work well together because they don't question each other's motivations. They accept each other unconditionally when it comes to why they're doing what they're doing. That's why they accept each other's suggestions. They are both inexplicably unorganized and super-humanely organized at the same time, and understand that about each other.

Blues enjoy interacting with each other because they travel to the same places to get their knowledge—all across the grid and into the ethers. No one can understand a blue like a blue. Blues have an easier acceptance of being taught by other blues than any other color and tend to trust what fellow blues say more. Sometimes, a blue will not be able to understand a concept or idea at all until it is explained by another blue. This is because they have the same reference points for what counts as wisdom.

Purples love each other's ability to give love. They love giving and receiving emotions and feeling what it feels like to be together. Because they want to be noticed and seen, purples tend to notice and see themselves in other purples—as though in a mirror. Because the appreciation of artistry is prized so highly by purples, they often find that only artists can create art up to their standards. These people may or may not be purples, but the group most certainly includes purples. In general, it takes a high level of mastery of your craft to gain the deep and abiding respect of a purple.

Finally, violets are good at giving each other the kindness and care that each seeks in the world. Violets appreciate each other's sensitivities, tastes, and the way each develops his or her life and the way they work with others. Multiple violets are often needed to work on the same project, and each can appreciate what the other contributes. At the end of the day, there is "so much to do," after all.

A person with your same master chakra can help you understand yourself better and can provide moral support for who you are and how you engage in the world. They constitute a unique kind of mirror. With so many shared experiences, it's hard to not be able to relate to another member of your master chakra. Some people even find it difficult to get angry at a member of their master chakra, someone of the same color, and typically will understand and excuse faults more readily. On the other hand, sometimes the biggest issues we can have with a color come from our very own.

A case in point is intimate relationships. Issues can arise when getting too close to your color. The exception to this rule is orange, who needs orange in order to stay on track when it comes to spiritual expansion.

Why can spending too much time with your own color create problems? When you date your own color, either literally or figuratively, you have the same strengths and weaknesses as your partner. Instead of reflecting back to you who you could be, you might both get stuck in your traps and stay there without knowing it. The reason why orange works well with orange is because oranges will actually verbalize which emotions their partner is feeling. No other color is good at observing traps to itself. Oranges are doing it together to make each other happy— this is why it can be reflexively done out of love. But often, when others who are the same color hang out, as in a romantic connection, one color must stop being itself for the other in order to maintain gender roles. For example, with two reds, you have two people that love to be the boss. This can create a crossroads. Who is going to be the boss in the relationship? One color will have to give up their core motivation of leadership to be follower to the other, sending them into a trap. Now we have a red behaving like a violet, and that isn't good for the red.

With yellow, there is *too* much thinking. It encourages yellows to stay in the trap of staying in their heads. No one is there to get them both out. With green, boredom ensues as two people who like to fix things and stand at the center of the chakra system, in a grounded position, attempt to create the polarity needed to sustain a long-term relationship. Next, blues, though they understand each other well, have the same ups and downs and tend to live too much in a mental realm when together. Where are the emotions? It is difficult for blues to not be in gifts and traps at the same time.

Purples can stagnate when together; and when purples join forces in a romantic relationship, there is a danger of them becoming narcissistic. Finally, when violets work together all the time, if they have to work on the same task, they will fight over it. Both looking to be told what to do, however, and both focused on completion, one needs to shade red to inspire the other to start, or take action in that realm.

## Reciprocal Chakras

These pairings represent good working partnerships and friendships, and are also considered best-case scenarios in terms of romantic relationships. Reciprocal colors work because they provide each other with what the other is missing without the effort of trying. As a tree breathes in carbon monoxide and exhales oxygen, your reciprocal color breathes out what you need, and breathes in what they need from you.

### Red * Violet

Violets will do what reds need done. Violets look to be told what to do at a level and to a degree that reds can accommodate. (Other colors do not want to tell the violets what to do *as* much; they would more so want the violet to think for themselves.) Violets will do the most for reds, who "do not do, but have it done." Violets are naturals at following the leader, though they are not limited to a role as follower. Still, they are the most likely to do what they are told without questioning, which helps reds in a crisis. Reds need the tenderness of the violet to assuage them and do something for them, as they spend much time in the battle-ready mode. Violets will make reds gentler, and reds tend to need a partner. Violets, as a rule, prefer to partner with others in order to live out their gift, and they need a partner the most of any gift. (Compare to yellow, who needs a partner the least of any gift.) Importantly, reds help violets manifest in the physical world. Reds start things; violets complete them. Violets, who are so tuned in to other people's needs, tend to feel safe and are happy being grounded around reds. Thus, violets and reds complete each other.

### Orange * Orange

Oranges "know how the game is played" and only another orange can play as well. This evens the playing field for both in the relationship. Oranges prefer to share leadership between themselves equally in a relationship, with sometimes one leading, then the other leading. It goes back and forth like two people playing catch. Other gifts might prefer that someone else be in control, more (for example, violets–reds, and blues–purples.) In any case, the dynamic is different. For those oranges who do engage in lying, cheating, and manipulation—a relationship with another orange will provide the proper checks and balances. Where other colors might feel betrayed by oranges' coming and going, in terms of their direction in life, other oranges would not. Most importantly, oranges act as mirrors to each other, allowing each other to choose feelings rather than simply give themselves over to them.

### Yellow * Green

Yellows tend to become scattered, and greens can clean up after them both physically and mentally. Yellows and greens can talk together at a high level of specificity and analytically regarding facts and the physical world, problems and how to solve them, and systems and how to set them up. Some other colors might find the depth of detail to be found in these conversations tedious. Yellows give the greens the truth, which the greens need in order to fix things or get their problems solved. And greens will not accept just any fix, but yellows can find the truth in a solution and bring to the table something that will and must satisfy a green. Also, yellows help greens to be less black and white—to see the higher concepts. Greens bring reason to yellows, who need to put pieces together to feel cohesive.

### Blue * Purple

Blues teach what the purples create; purples supply the blues with material for them to teach so they don't always have to go and find another source, though this is something blues would never stop doing. Purples provide an idea, and blues expand upon it and make the vision bigger. Purples tend to get caught up in what they are doing and neglect the bigger picture, which blues are all about. Purples and blues both like to travel—on the earth and on spiritual planes. Purples can go where the blues travel to obtain their knowledge and give them love. Blues go where the purples come from and give them structure and knowledge and ideas to build on. Purples like how blues think and understand them. Blues are on a high mental plane, and need purples' divine love to soften them. Blues can be mean, but purples can love them or manipulate them back into place; purples can be myopic, focusing too much on self, and blues can spot it and bring them back to their hearts. Blues are able to be dispassionate when purples feel out of control. This provides checks and balances when we're in our off states. On the best days, a dance of wisdom and love occurs between them, as blues engage and enlarge the purple's visions. Blues respond to purples' artistic direction with spontaneity and an inner knowing of what they are trying to do. Not every color can keep up with blues, who have the most endurance and are constantly traveling to other dimensions and planes. Purples can go there. Purples give so much love they sometimes wonder why no one gives it back—but blues, whose love is of passionate giving, give just as much back as purples want.

Even though there is an ideal master chakra partner for everyone, any color can be in a successful relationship with any other as long as the partners can accept and heal each other. It's important to learn how to work with each of the colors because we are meant to contribute to each other's lives by interacting across the spectrum.

However, knowing yourself is the first step to deepening your connection with others. Your newfound knowledge of your master chakra, your divine light, can help you express and accept yourself more on target. Therefore, let's first strengthen your ability to be you. You can embrace the light over the darkness and be who you truly are. The next section, workbooks for each chakra, helps you see how you can be yourself more happily.

# 11

# THE MASTER CHAKRA WORKBOOKS

The workbooks for each spiritual gift help you explore your area of giftedness, letting you expand your service to the world. They help you develop awareness about the gift you already have so you can identify its aspects. If you are going to live in your light, you must know what that light refers to. If you are conflicted about giving your gift, writing answers to the questions will unlock doors for you that await opening. The questions also aim to assist you in treating yourself, your mind, and your instincts with more respect for its proclivities, so that you can give your gift with confidence and an awareness of what it really means. Working on your master chakra is ultimately an act of justice toward you and your mind; it will affect each human being you come into contact with in ways you cannot imagine. You are going into the unknown, into the beyond, into the interstices between darkness and light in order to turn on the lights not only for yourself, to keep you alive, but for others—to be a candle in their dark night of the soul. So, it's silly to understate the importance of your work on your own soul. You cannot bring about a better state of things, unless you figure out how to become whole yourself. But you cannot do that unless or until you realize your own power and breadth of understanding. To do that, you have to know who you are, and that includes who you were.

Giving your master chakra gift to yourself provides you with needed nourishment that can enable you to be a more confident, happy, and even healthy person within the confines of this awareness. For one thing, doing it regularly gets you out of your traps. This workbook is the place where you find out more about how to move through your traps with acumen. It will inspire you to come up with even more ways to emerge back on your path from any dark space you might have gone into.

Sometimes we give away our power. These workbooks help you reclaim what was yours, which various state-like imperialistic and anti-holistic agencies have taken from you. To take it back and realize that you can give all of your helpfulness in your master chakra to others in ways that will work for them is only going to create a better system. Not only that, but because other people know you better than yourself, why not get to know them and work through their workbooks, too? If you are in your traps, you'll begin to define how and why certain issues can detract from your purpose once you complete your own workbook. Now, our ego serves us in very important ways, and it needs to be healthy for us to proceed with caution, as we often must do. When the ego is overactive, or reactive (in fear), we go into our traps. It is possible to overcome your traps completely, though. Doing so is not easy, and could take a long time. Yet the more you practice your gifts, the less you will go to your traps.

Your workbook questions help you zero in on where you need more awareness of your greatness and where you could make adjustments to improve how you handle your ego and your shadow side. Too often I find people's spiritual gifts lying dormant because of fear. So, this is an opportunity to acknowledge what anyone has not been doing, and what they can be doing more of. How you use your spiritual sustenance is up to you. These questions give you pointers to walking the path more securely within your own light as you find the best ways to support yourself as a spiritual, not just a material being. Please refer to the information in the chapters about each master chakra, and in the Appendix to remind yourself what each of these chakra functions entail, to enrich your reflections upon them. Remember, no one is making you do this. That's why it's called a spiritual, and not a religious path. At every step, the choice is yours to take the rainbow bridge or focus on the past.

# 12

# RED WORKBOOK

## A Physical-Physical Spiritual Gift, Feminine in Nature: The Natural Leader

*You might be a red if...*

+ You like tradition and sometimes, the good old days when people had more structure and listened to authority, had handguns in their holsters, and looked people in the eye—even taking justice into their own hands in its time, without waiting for the government to intervene and mess it up.

+ You're a "back in the day" kind of person. You wish people would get up to speed with the old ways.

+ You dislike politics, because in that world it can be difficult to take action. You might come to the world of politics from another arena in order to bypass the way things are ordinarily done so that you can get something done.

+ You don't like it when anyone infringes on the power of an individual to choose their own way of being in the world.

+ You want things done your way, in any case, and think people should do them your way.

+ You get things moving.

+ You attract people into your circle nearly every day.

+ You push yourself to win, and when everyone does, you're on cloud nine.

+ You show people to the finish line and into their greatness. You let them accomplish things they couldn't accomplish without leadership toward that star.

+ You love people for who they are, but care most about what they do or don't do.

+ You can laugh if something doesn't work out.

+ You think safety comes first.

+ You judge by the physical. It's your tool of the trade. It's your reason for living.

+ You work hard.

+ You love doing things that push your boundaries.

+ You use your instincts and intuition and insist that others do, too.

+ You might punish people for deserving you and your leadership because you believe you're just that awesome. However, you don't like it when other people put you on a pedestal.

+ You take things to the next level.

+ You put a stop to bullying.

+ People look up to you.

### When in their giftedness, reds tend to ...
(According to Joseph Crane)

+ Be pioneers.

+ Run businesses.

+ Use their intuition to lead.

+ Be intuitive.

+ Show the way—take someone to a better place.

- Prepare the way—take a group in action and take responsibility for the result. (For reds, it is about the group/others, not about themselves.)

- Be responsible and accountable; they do not blame.

- Protect the people they lead.

- Take the heat, pay the price.

- Silently score results, but the glory is when everyone wins.

- Be physical in nature—they judge by the physical. They ask: "did it show up? Did it happen? If so, then it worked. If not, then what happened?"

*When in their traps, reds tend to ...*
*(According to Joseph Crane)*

- Be egotistical.

- Be stubborn, immovable.

- Be power hungry.

- Take no responsibility for the action or non-action.

- Order others around or rule using fear.

- Use others as tools.

- Make it ALL about them, "Look at what I have done." Glory is for themselves.

+ Play the victim, blaming everyone but themselves.

+ Whine.

+ Believe lies others tell them about themselves.

## Reflection Questions

The following questions will help you explore your gift and determine how to use it to your advantage in the world.

While answering these questions, refer back to the information you just read about the gifts and traps as necessary.

1. You and your soul-ray color are both gifts, and as such, have gifts to share with the world. This makes you a master, or an expert, on how this gift is played out. How do you see yourself being in your gifts?

2. Which aspects of your gift seem new to you? (Maybe you've never thought about them before.)

3. Which aspects of your gifts would you like to use better, now that you've become aware they exist?

4. What traps do you currently struggle with in your life?

5. Can you identify triggers that move you into your traps?

6. The way out of any red trap for a red is to "listen to what God is telling you and know the power you are." How would your life change if you did this often?

7. Can you set a goal to become good at recognizing when you are in your gifts, and when you are in your traps? How long do you think it would take? Which do you want to accomplish first?

8. Do you have any insights about what it is like to be red? No one knows your gift like you! Please share your insights.

9. Reds need to create goals so that they can maintain focus and do not feel scattered. This helps a red feel more on point. Also, the more action taken toward achieving a goal, the better the red feels as this moves him or her into action and out of the trap of inaction. Goals and action plans for achieving them (necessary steps to take) are essential to this process. Brainstorm some goals you could create to move your life forward at this time.

10. Goals can come in many sizes. Larger goals take a longer time period to achieve and may entail intermittent goals along the path there. Write the three goals that resonate with you most from your brainstorming list. Then, write down smaller subgoals or action steps you will need to accomplish to achieve the larger goals.

11. Reds go through stages in their life: When they are young, they often seek power for themselves and to control through power and force. When they are older, they become less interested in this and more interested

in leading from the heart. Where are you right now? Where would you like to be?

12. The red gift, which is physical-physical, draws from the physical realm. It is also a highly intuitive gift. Many reds have advised that they lead from behind rather than from out in front. They like to inspire people to do their best and tell them what to do as well. Given all of this, this gift is feminine in nature. Since thinking of the gift of leadership as feminine is a new idea, and goes against the stereotype of leaders as masculine, please reflect on how *you* see your gift as being feminine or blending with the feminine. Remember, each person, whether man or woman, has a masculine and feminine side.

13. Reds often do well when they have violet friends. Violets will help reds be gentler, in addition to helping them with anything they have to do. Read about the violet gift and reflect on its value.

14. Do you know any violets? How can you tell?

15. Describe what you have noticed about what it's like for you to interact with violets in your life. What do they do for you? What can you do for them?

16. Reds are often left responsible for what does or doesn't occur around them, whether they like it or not. That's because you are a natural leader, and the natural leader's

job is to make things happen and go in the right direction. It's important not to take credit for things that you
didn't do, but it's also good to take responsibility when
you didn't do something that you could have done.
Do you ever blame others when things don't happen
the way you see they should? How can you take more
responsibility for what happens around you? How can
you improve sharing your leadership with others?

17. Reds need followers because it's very hard to get things
    done when no one helps you; reds prefer to take
    charge of a big picture, rather than a small detail. It's
    the other people around him or her who trust him or
    her, who actually do most of the work (though not all
    of it!). Can you think of a time when you created a big
    picture, pitched into help, but it was other people you
    organized around you who really helped you to make
    the grade, and complete the project?

18. Using your knowledge of the red-violet connection,
    which you learned about in the Light Partners chapter,
    reflect on its importance for you. How have you expe-
    rienced your relationships with violets in years gone
    by? How would being in good standing with violets
    help you improve your lifestyle?

19. Reds and violets make good friends, colleagues, and
    also ideal romantic partners, due to this dynamic.
    Once again, reflect on the observations above and how

you have experienced the red–violet connection over the years. How could it get even better?

20. How do you feel about being a red? What it is like? What do you like about it? If you were to describe your master chakra to someone else to let them know what it is like, what would you say?

21. Honoring your gift is very important. The more you honor it in yourself, the more others will honor it in you, and the less likely you are to be walked on or your gifts disregarded. You will gain more respect for who you are and your light will shine brighter because these things will be present in you. In fact, they already are in a much deeper way simply because you've engaged this much with this information so far. What commitment are you willing to make regarding honoring yourself in the future?

22. How can you honor yourself for your own greatness?

23. Envision by drawing or writing what it means to be a red and what you will accomplish in the future with your gifts.

## Daily Practices

You can continue these practices as long as you wish to check yourself as you become more aware of your giftedness. The more aware you are of how you live in your gifts, versus not, the more you'll be able to emerge from traps and their associated consequences.

### Reflection on your soul-ray color...

1. In what ways did you live out your gift today? Be specific. (For an advanced practice, you might consider how you shaded into the two master chakras on either side of you to be in your gifts.)

2. Did you catch yourself going into any traps today? Were you able to avoid any traps?

3. Are you in a trap in this moment, now that you think about it? If so, what would you like to do about it? Make a commitment. Either give your gift back to yourself now or take action promptly to return to your gifted awareness.

4. Simply coming into awareness of who and what you are as a master of one of the seven spiritual chakras can be the first step toward being able to stay in the light of your own self, with no one to hinder you. If you memorize your gifts and traps, you'll know when you are in one versus the other and how to walk with your connection with the divine. You can find the best exits for your traps in the paragraph below.

Because reds can shade violet or orange once in a while, you can get stuck in a trap of either of these two colors. They are right next to yours on the chakra system.

*List of exits from red's traps …*

+ Use your intuition to tell you what is needed in a situation where you don't feel at your best.

+ Ask yourself what you need right now.

+ Give yourself mercy and compassion (violet).

+ Listen to what God is telling you and know the power you are (red).

+ Give yourself the gift of joy from within (orange).

## More Aspects of Your Gift

Now, let's talk more about that aspect of being a red, which is that reds can shade violet and orange in order to live out their gifts. Reflect now on how, why, or when you shade violet and orange. Read the description of violets in their giftedness and then answer the questions below.

1. When do you most often find yourself using your violet?

2. Could you expand this ability to serve a purpose?

Reds like to use their fun side to get people involved in working toward goals. They, who are so good at running businesses, need to be able to promote it. Having special access to orange makes this easier.

While no one is an orange like an orange, reds can be very familiar with orange by close proximity. (The sacral and the root chakras are right next to each other.) Read the description of oranges in their giftedness and reflect on how you use it to be less serious for yourself, and others, in time.

1. When do you most often find yourself using your orange gift?

2. Could you expand this ability to serve a purpose?

## Meditation to Remember Who You Truly Are

The following meditation will assist you in exiting from any of the red traps:

> Visualize your pranic tube, a column of white light that runs through the middle of your body, up to Source, and intend to feel the love of God coming through it. Feel the love of God, feel yourself loving God through your pranic tube.

> This white light energy may expand outward to encompass you.

> See yourself listening to God. Listen to what God is telling you. Wait until you receive a download or message. Even if you feel you do not know what the message is yet, you will know when you have received information. It will unfold later if not now.

Be saturated with the power you are as you listen to what God is telling you.

Do not exit the meditation until you feel filled with the power you are and have fully listened to what God is telling you.

**This meditation works!** Do it as often as possible when you feel you lack purpose or direction, or find yourself in any trap.

## Purification Process
*To release the effects of the lies, manipulation of others*
A major problem for a red can crop up when they accept someone else's truth in place of their own—and then end up following that lead, instead of building their own way forward based on none other than their own point of view. It's okay to be influenced, but not led by the nose. If what someone else says does not match your own compass, it's time to consider the source.

We have all gone along with what someone else said, and hence failed to lead our own lives. For reds, it's more serious, because when they fail to step up to the plate, it affects the group at large, everyone who could benefit from their point of view. Grabbing onto the thoughts of others to keep from drowning is not keeping your eye on the ball. When a red uses external ideas as a plan instead of their own intuitive guidance to create a new way forward, it impoverishes us all.

Use this exercise to release the energy of manipulation and return to a space from which you can connect to God and bring in the power you are. You will need some supplies to complete the ceremony below: a bundle of sage and some matches.

Go to a clean place. Be in a state of mind in connection with God. When you are at peace, in quiet, then begin.

Take the sage and burn it. Put it all around you. To the right, to the left, above, and below. Get on one knee.

Say: *I solemnly ask to be purified from the emotions of others*

*As they relate to things which are not of me.*

*In terms of direction, I ask*

*That I be purified from all impurities of the will of anyone less than God.*

*I am love, I am light, I am Source. I am at one with God.*

*I am divine source in all its wonderment and talents.*

*My skills, abilities, and talents support me in the world.*

*They are God-given, and no other can come between.*

*I am the I am.*

*I can think for myself all things above and below*

*Which direct me to direct the will of others in a kind and loving manner.*

*With my skills, abilities, and talents*

*With my Source*

*I cannot fail in the living of this, my light.*

*And so it is.*

Your prayer will be carried to heaven.

Put out the sage.

Once you have answered all of the workbook questions, applied what you've learned in your daily living, and used the meditations, reflect on how far you've come and how much you've grown. Can you think of other things to do, outside this workbook, that will help you expand how you use your gifts to increase awareness and raise consciousness, for the benefit of all?

# 13

# ORANGE WORKBOOK

**A Physical-Emotional Spiritual Gift,
Feminine in Nature, the Natural Joy-Bringer**
*You might be an orange if …*

+ You say yes to opposing parties and an abundance
  of requests or deals.

+ Sometimes you make it all happen and blow
  people away.

+ You like to take gambles.

+ It's really all about you.

+ You're great at selling something or moving someone into action, getting them to go along with what you suggest.

+ You don't want to do something so you just don't do it.

+ You talk to the person no one else is talking to.

+ You like everyone (except the downers—but you strive to make them happy anyway).

+ You get people involved in activities—with each other, or in social events like parties, concerts, skydiving, dancing, volleyball tournaments, or any kind of thing you think is fun.

+ You give your exclusive time and energy to a person when you are with them.

+ You lift people out of a dark hole frequently.

+ People say you are too happy.

+ You make other people happy so you can be happy.

+ You poke and prod people so they'll talk. You then listen during that conversation for the place where the tempo picks up. You enjoy talking to people about themselves until they feel upbeat again. Then you extend the conversation from there.

+ Life is all about having fun and enjoying it, usually
  with a bunch of people. (That's not boring.)

+ You prize spontaneity.

+ You're good at finding fun things to do.

+ You break dates for better dates.

+ You love to dance.

+ You define fun for others. (You determine what
  fun even is.)

+ You make instant friends.

+ You break rules when necessary to unleash the
  joy inside.

+ You think rules were made for breaking!

+ You'll embarrass someone to make them laugh,
  but you'll make yourself look silly just to help
  them out.

+ You spend money easily because you know it will
  come back to you.

+ You skip town when people are depressing.

+ If someone hurts you and you can't find a way
  out, you'll hurt them extra to make sure they can't
  come back and hurt you again, because it's too
  hard to be happy when that happens.

+ You need your alone time.

+ You analyze situations and look at aspects of the human dynamics involved to figure out how to maneuver.

+ You know how the game is played, and you play it well.

+ You love to have fun, be fun, and to cause love.

## When in their giftedness, oranges tend to ...
*(According to Joseph Crane)*

+ Be people persons—enjoying dining, talking, smiling, and rah-rah let's have a good time people.

+ Be promoters—they go out and get everyone excited about what it is you are doing.

+ Be extremely fun people to be around.

+ Give out of joy and for the happiness of others.

+ Support others.

+ Defend those they love.

+ Embrace a healthy lifestyle.

+ Be emotional, generous, and giving.

+ Embrace duality and see both sides of everything.

+ Be bubbly, exciting, and stand out!

+ Raise your standard to greatness.

+ Believe life is a party, and they are not always in touch with reality.

+ Be gamblers and do well in real estate.

## When in their traps oranges, tend to ...
*(According to Joseph Crane)*

+ Believe it's all about *them* and how *they* feel about it.

+ Constantly look for excitement and something to feed their emotions.

+ Not stick with something long enough because of lack of focus.

+ Get caught up in their traps, and they become confused and overanalyze their feelings.

+ Get too caught up in their emotions.

+ Become judgmental.

+ Blame others.

+ Give you their advice, which is not good advice because it is based on feelings of the moment.

+ Destroy a relationship the easiest by saying exactly how they feel.

## Reflection Questions

The following are contemplation questions to help you explore your orange gift, know yourself, and improve. While answering these questions, refer back to the information you just read about the gifts and traps as necessary.

1. You and your soul-ray color are both gifts, and as such, have gifts to share with the world. This makes you a master, or expert, on how this gift is done. How do you see yourself living in your gifts?

2. Which aspects of your gift seem new to you? (Maybe you've never thought about them before.)

3. Which aspects of your gift would you like to embrace more fully now that you are consciously aware that you have special access to them? What would be the result?

4. What traps do you struggle with in your life at this time?

5. Can you identify triggers that move you into any of these traps? Which triggers move you into which traps?

6. The way out of a trap for an orange is to give yourself divine love and joy. What do you think this means? How would your life change if you did this often?

7. Can you set a goal to become good at recognizing when you are in your gifts, and when you are in your traps? Which do you want to accomplish first? How long do you think it would take?

8. What questions do you have about your gift?

9. Do you have any insights about what it is like to have this gift? No one knows your gift like you! Please share your insights below.

The following questions were written by Kim Brushaber, an orange good at sharing with other oranges how they can grow.

10. One of oranges' greatest joys in life is to help uplift and inspire others. This becomes increasingly difficult to do when you are in your traps and not feeling like your regular bubbly self. Many oranges isolate themselves from others when they are depressed, and it can frequently take another orange (orange's helper color) to help them get out of their funk. What happens to you when you are in a funk? Why do you think you feel that way? What happens to other people around you?

11. Oranges love to uplift other people. However, we discover that not everyone wants to or can be uplifted. Oranges will frequently criticize or blame others when they work hard at uplifting someone who is unwilling to budge. What do you do in these circumstances? How could you react differently? Are there people in your life that you really should let go of?

12. Oranges love to chase the fun stuff. Frequently this causes an orange to overbook their social arrangements.

Oranges will pick whatever sounds like the most fun in the moment. Unfortunately, this makes them appear to be rather flaky or over committed at times. How can you balance your schedule better in order to ensure that no one is left sad when you don't show up at their party? What can you do differently so that you don't feel pulled in so many different directions?

13. One of the greatest joys in an orange's life is making someone's life even better after they've left it. This has sometimes come at a cost of sacrificing your own happiness. Are there places in your life where you should draw boundaries? What are you doing to inspire your own happiness? What would you say to yourself to uplift you? What makes you happy that has nothing to do with other people?

14. Oranges are viewed by others as the everlasting energizer bunny. Keeping the party going and everyone happy takes a lot of work. One way to recharge is to find another orange. Do you have a list of other oranges in your life who can help to recharge you? What do you do to recharge yourself?

15. Oranges are perfect at seeing the silver lining in everything. It's very uncomfortable for an orange to stay in a bad mood for very long. How do you handle negative emotions? How do you handle other people's negative emotions?

16. Oranges get bored easily. It's part of our nature to do whatever seems like the most fun, and if it isn't fun it isn't worth doing. Unfortunately, much of life is boring. Oranges do whatever they can to make a moment interesting, but it's not always appropriate to do so. How do you handle the boring things in your life? Is there a better way for you to handle them?

Oranges spend so much time making other people happy. Sometimes, it's taken for granted. If you have conditioned people around you to depend on you, they can react negatively when you take your sunshine away. People may call you selfish if you take time for yourself. People may not take you seriously. Other people's negative comments about you can be very devastating when all you are trying to do is bring joy and happiness to everyone around you. How does being orange impact other people's perceptions about you?

17. Can you see how other people's judgments about you are actually about themselves more than they are about you?

18. How do you deal with these situations as they come up?

19. How can you react while maintaining your positive orange attitude?

20. Oranges are naturally the life of the party. They light up the room when they come in. Everyone is their friend. Have you ever taken a moment to really understand

what a gift that is that you bring to others? Have you been complimented on your stories? your jokes? your dancing? your laugh? Do you realize what you bring to people around you when you are in your gifts?

21. Oranges help people shift from a bad situation to a good one. Change is not an easy thing for most people. Oranges intuitively know what to say or do to make someone's life better. We do it naturally without even knowing we're doing it. Like George Bailey said in *It's a Wonderful Life*, we affect people every single day. Have you taken a moment to recognize the good that you do for everyone around you? How have you inspired someone this week? Write about those experiences.

22. For oranges, rules are made to be broken—but only in the name of fun. What rules have you broken that were meant to be broken?

23. What rules have you broken that you have regretted?

24. What rules do you wish that you could go back and break?

Now, back to my questions about the orange master chakra.

25. One major thing another orange can do for you is mirror what you are feeling so you can decide what you want to feel. Can you see how this might make it easier

to adjust your course? Describe any other oranges you have known and what they did for you.

26. Now, review the observations about how oranges benefit from each other's presence in relationships in the Light Partners chapter.

What is your reaction to this information?

27. Reciprocal colors, such as orange and orange, provide each other with what the other is missing without the effort of trying. This is why they are considered best-case scenarios when it comes to romantic relationships. What are some insights you have about this?

28. How do you feel about being orange? What is it like? What do you like the best about it? the least about it? What would you like to change? If you were to describe your gift to someone else, what would you say?

29. Honoring your gift is very important. The more you honor it in yourself, the more others will honor it in you. The less you are to be walked on or your gifts disregarded. You will gain more respect for who you are and your light will shine more brightly, because these things will be present in you. In fact, they already are in a much deeper way simply because you've engaged with this information so far. What commitment are you willing to make regarding honoring yourself?

30. How can you honor yourself for your own greatness?

31. Envision by drawing or writing what it means to be an orange and what you will accomplish in the future with your gifts.

## Daily Practices

The following sequence of questions will help you notice your gifts more and how you share them. It will help you grow in your light, the light of who you are, and avoid pitfalls you may be experiencing on a large scale. You can continue these practices as long as you wish to check your awareness about living in your giftedness—your special way of bringing joy to those around you. The more aware you are, the more you will be able to avoid your traps and their associated consequences. Realize that traps are not bad; still, they will feel inconvenient or unpleasant. The goal is to learn from the experience of being in your trap, and notice when you are in one, and then choose to return to the best part of you.

*Reflection on your soul-ray color...*

1. In what ways did you live out of your gift today? Be specific. Please refer to the beginning of this workbook and the descriptions of your gifts and traps when completing this section.

2. Did you catch yourself going into any traps today? Were you able to avoid these traps?

3. Are you in a trap now and not aware of it? If so, what would you like to do about it? Make a decision and a commitment now. Either give yourself your gift right here and now, or make a decision to take action in this regard tomorrow.

4. Remembering who and what you are as a master of the clear chakra—orange—is the first step toward being able to securely remain in the light of your own power. If you memorize your gifts and traps, you'll know when you are in one versus the other and how to slide back into your connection with the divine, otherwise known as the best exit for your trap, which is listed below.

The following list is a reminder of how to exit from the orange traps. Because oranges can shade to the two colors right next to them, red and yellow, once in a while, they will get stuck in the trap of one of these colors. If you suspect this is happening, you may use the list to remember how to remove yourself from the trap of the other color.

*List of exits from orange's traps . . .*

+ Use your intuition to tell you what is needed in a situation where you don't feel at your best.

+ Ask yourself what you need right now.

+ Listen to what God is telling you and know the power you are (red).

+ Open your heart to the divine love you hold for others (orange).

+ Connect to your ability to naturally know and reason (yellow).

## More Aspects of Your Gift

Now, let's talk more about that aspect of being an orange, which is that oranges can shade the territory of red and yellow in order to live out their gifts. Reflect on how, why, and when you shade red and yellow. Read the description of reds in their giftedness and then answer the questions below.

1. When do you most often find yourself utilizing red?

2. If you need to be red, you can be. When might it be good to shade red?

Oranges are especially good at using their yellow gift to analyze what is going on for their own future plans and even to help others enjoy life more. Explore your yellow side by thinking about the following description and how it applies to you. (Read the description of yellows in their giftedness.)

1. When do you most often find yourself utilizing yellow?

2. If you need to be yellow, you can be. When might it be beneficial to shade yellow?

To help yourself return to your joy, please use the meditation on "Being Joy" in the violet workbook. It walks you through how to return to your nice orange self if you're out of touch with the true reality of how happy you are.

## Releasing Anxiety

Sometimes you have trouble releasing your baggage. All the energy you have can sometimes get backed up and you don't know what to do with it. The burden of making others feel happy can make you feel as though you are responsible for others. This exercise follows the orange energy pattern of bubbles, which has you releasing your worries and cares through balloons.

It's a sunny day. You are in a room, and you leave to go outside. You put your feet in the grass. The yellow dandelions look bright and sunny against your bare feet as you lean against the bike rack.

To the bike rack are tied innumerable orange balloons. You choose one.

Into this balloon, you put something you no longer desire to carry with you on your journey.

You let it go.

You take another balloon. Into this balloon, you place a worry or a care.

The balloon sails high up into the air until you can no longer see it.

You take another balloon, and that balloon contains another thought you no longer wish to have.

You let it go.

You take a fourth balloon and put something else into it you crave to let go.

There are as many balloons as you need to handle stress, fears, struggles, and tiredness. You keep placing these types of things into the balloons until you are finished and you don't have any more of them left.

As you let go of each balloon, you feel a little lighter.

And a little lighter.

Until, when you are totally finished, you brush off your hands and take a step forward.

Now, you feel even lighter than ever before and are ready to face the world.

# 14

# Yellow Workbook

### A Physical-Mental Gift, Masculine in Nature: The Natural Thinker

*You might be a yellow if...*

+ Data is your best friend.

+ You need to know the truth and must find it to survive.

+ You reach for the stars. Your goals are big and they stretch over extremely long time frames.

+ You often take things literally.

+ Everyone else laughs at the joke you can't understand.

- You can be unemotional when called for. It lets you think and process beyond all comprehension of smaller minds.

- You can be sneaky when needed, passive as a rule, and funny. But usually, you're just serene.

- You share facts with your people, and strive to act in accordance with all you know.

- You find out the truth even when other people are hiding it from you.

- You can be fun, friendly, and gregarious when the moment strikes, and the situation has you happy.

- Other people seek you out so you can solve their problems. In like manner, you approach others with an interest in what they can do for you.

- You meet others on the mental plane for a clear discussion of genius.

- You ask a lot of questions. You hold back the class with your questions.

- You don't lie if you can possibly avoid it.

- You like to give people information about how they can best do things. These well-meaning talks and lectures are based on what you've observed about how things work in the world at large.

- The topic at hand is infinitely observable in all times, in all places, and in all faces.

- Your questions find the various angles you need to lift the clearest assessments out of what other people hold as true. From there, you'll make an assessment based on what you already know.

- You feel a truth for its vibration and know how right it is or isn't.

- Without meaning to, you will say truthful things that hurt people, and sometimes, things that are amazing and wonderful for them to hear, because while other people can hide the truth without knowing they are doing that, you always reveal it unintentionally, if not intentionally.

- The truth can hurt, but since it's your area, you don't worry about it.

- Less imminent, but still cogent, is how the truth heals and flies in the face of anything that people have done up to this point.

- You want to spend all of your time thinking.

- You love to invent solutions to your problems, because for one thing, they don't exist yet.

- It takes you a long time to process new information.

+ Like Heidi Shelton-Oliver says, you sure don't take things at face value.

+ You can't stand the untruth, the lies, and the deception of modern life.

+ You can be your own best friend because you know what it means to have a friend and be one to. You achieve mastery of friendship and can talk to anyone from a place of love.

+ You are a master of stoicity when less emotional, and of focus when you are kind.

+ You face adversity unlike any other color: without any mystery, like iron in the forge.

+ You wish others to know how great you are by your limitless ambitions.

+ You seek accuracy in all things and make decisions based upon it.

+ You will ask questions of yourself if no one is around.

+ You laugh at the follies of man.

*When in their giftedness, yellows tend to ...*
(*According to Joseph Crane*)

+ Be thinkers—they come up with the ideas.

+ Be great research and development people.

+ Take in data and process it.

+ Be mental in nature and very good at it.

+ Be philosophers—higher mind, natural knowing.

+ Be intellectual—develop conscious thought.

+ Be seekers of truth.

+ Be holders of great knowledge.

+ Analyze anything and come up with a better way.

+ Be forgiving because they can reason it out and understand why you did what you did.

+ Not be emotional.

+ Not let emotions get in the way of their thinking.

### When in their traps, yellows tend to ...
*(According to Joseph Crane)*

+ Be all about the mental process.

+ Think that others are stupid and unable to grasp the simplest concepts.

+ Have forgotten the gift they have.

+ Close themselves off from others.

+ Be cold and unforgiving.

✦ Absolutely not deal with their feelings.

✦ Stay in their heads to avoid feelings and avoid being hurt.

✦ Lose contact with the real world, staying in their heads and their idealism.

## Reflection Questions

While answering these questions, refer back to the information you just read about the gifts and traps as necessary.

1. You and your soul-ray color are both gifts, and as such, you have gifts to share with the world. This makes you a master, or expert, on how your yellow research gift works. How do you see yourself working in your gift-edness on behalf of yourself?

2. Which aspects of your gift seem new to you? (Maybe you've never thought about them before.)

3. Which aspects of your gift would you like to embrace more fully now that you are consciously aware that you have special access to them? What would be the result?

4. Which traps do you struggle with, currently, in your daily life?

5. Can you identify triggers that move you into your traps?

6. Can you set a goal to become good at recognizing when you are in your gifts, and when you are in your

traps? How long do you think it would take? Which do you want to accomplish first?

7. What questions do you have about your gift?

8. Do you have any insights about what it is like to have this gift? No one knows your gift like you! Please share your insights.

9. The way out of a trap for a yellow is to "connect with your consciousness of reason and natural knowing." What does this mean to you?

10. Natural knowing means seeing how things work together in a process-oriented way. It means making observations of the world and how things work. How often do you do this?

11. Natural knowing also refers to a person's intuitive senses. How often are you aware of what your senses tell you?

12. How would your life change if you often connected to your intuition, focusing on how things worked?

13. Could you do it more? In what areas?

14. What is a good standard of reason?

15. What does being "reasonable" mean to you?

16. How often are you aware of what is reasonable?

17. Do you think you need to improve your ability to perceive what is reasonable and apply it to how you make decisions? In what areas? What actions could you take? What resources might you seek?

18. How could you improve your evaluation on what is reasonable?

There is a meditation on connecting to your natural knowing and ability to reason at the end of this workbook. It walks you through doing both in an energetic way, making it easier for you to get in the habit of.

19. Yellows can feel scattered at times. What happens to this feeling when you focus?

20. The scattered feeling of a yellow can be reflected externally in their environment. What happens to your feeling of being scattered when you clean up your surroundings? How does it feel to be a yellow?

21. Yellows can neglect the emotional aspect. How do you include emotion in your life? How could you do better?

22. If you were to allow emotion to play a bigger role in your life, what would you do? Who would you talk to?

23. What would studying emotions as a research topic do for your life?

24. What are three benefits you can think of to make sure you feel your emotions every day?

25. What are the benefits of being social regularly or learning how to be (experimenting?)

26. Yellows often do well when they have green friends. Greens help yellows be less scattered in addition to giving them constant problems to work through and work out! Greens provide yellows with the expertise in fixing things that they find don't work well in the world or are based on untruth. Read about the green gift in the appendix, which gives an overview of all the soul-ray colors, and reflect on its value here.

27. Do you know any greens? How can you tell? (What are the telling characteristics?)

28. Describe what you have noticed about interacting with greens in your life. What do they do for you? What can you do for them?

29. Now, review the observations in the Light Partner chapter about how greens and yellows need each other. While you do not need a green to complete you, the green gift can enhance a yellow gift. Speculate on what it might be like to associate with a green regularly as a friend. Why might that be appropriate for your growth? What do you imagine it could be like? How could it improve your lifestyle?

30. Yellows and greens make good friends and colleagues, but also ideal romantic partners due to this dynamic.

You can learn more about it in the Reciprocal Colors section of the Light Partners chapter. What are some insights you have about this interaction?

31. Back to you. How do you feel about being yellow? What is it like? What do you like the best about it? If you were to describe your gift to someone else, to let them know what it is like, what would you say?

32. Honoring your gift is very important. The more you honor it in yourself, the more others will honor it in you. The less likely you are to be walked on or your gifts disregarded. You will gain more respect for who you are and your light will shine brighter because these things will be present in you. In fact, they already are in a much deeper way simply because you've engaged this much with this information so far. What commitment are you willing to make regarding honoring yourself in the future?

33. How can you honor yourself for your own greatness?

34. Envision by drawing or writing what it means to be a yellow and what you will accomplish in the future with your gifts.

## Daily Practices

The following sequence of questions will help you notice your gifts more and how you share them. It will help you grow in your light, the light of who you are, and avoid pitfalls you may have been experiencing on a large scale. One can continue these practices as long as one wishes as a self-check to raise awareness about living in giftedness—your special way of living in the light. The more aware you are, the more you will be able to avoid your traps and their associated consequences.

*Reflection on your soul-ray color:*

1. In what ways did you live out of your gift today? Be specific.

2. Did you catch yourself going into any traps today? Were you able to avoid these traps?

3. Are you in a trap now and not aware of it? If so, what would you like to do about it? Make a decision and a commitment now. Make a decision. Give yourself your gift in the moment. See what happens!

4. Simply coming into awareness of your gifts and traps is a large feat in the beginning. Consider memorizing your gifts and traps in order to be able to know the nuances and when you must shift from one to the other.

Because yellows can shade orange or green once in a while, you will get stuck in a trap of either of these two colors. If you suspect this is happening, you may use the list below to remember how to remove yourself from the trap of the other color.

*List of exits from yellow's traps …*

- ✦ Use your intuition to tell you what is needed in a situation where you don't feel at your best.

- ✦ Ask yourself what you need right now.

- ✦ Give yourself joy (orange).

- ✦ Connect to your natural knowing and ability to reason (yellow).

- ✦ Give anything you give because of the love of God (green).

## More Aspects of Your Gift

Now, let's talk more about that aspect of being a yellow, which is that yellows can shade orange and green in order to live out their gifts.

Reflect now on how, why, or when you shade orange and green. Read the description of oranges in their giftedness and then answer the questions.

1. When do you most often find yourself utilizing orange?

2. Could you expand this ability to serve a purpose?

While no one is a green like a green, yellows can be very familiar with greens by close proximity (the solar plexus and heart chakras are right next to each other). Now, let's explore your green side. Read the description of greens in their giftedness and then answer the questions.

1. When do you most often find yourself using your green?

2. Could you expand this ability to serve a purpose?

When you find yourself going into your traps, the following meditation can assist. This meditation is merely a guide; once you have the concept and the feeling of what happens here, you may not need to use the entire meditation as thoroughly as it's described. Here is a way to be thorough in the exiting of your trap.

## Meditation to Connect with Natural Knowing

Sit with your feet flat on the floor and your hands on your lap, palm up. Now, raise one hand as though you were motioning someone to stop, but relax your arm. This allows energy to flow freely. Uninhibited, emotions will come in.

Now, take the other hand and touch your middle finger to your thumb. You can raise your arm off your lap to do this.

Close your eyes. Imagine your crown chakra; it looks like a lotus. Let the lotus flower bloom there.

Now, visualize your left brain. See yourself there in your analytical mind, thinking. See your consciousness move from your left brain down your head, through your neck, and to your heart. Your consciousness is now at the heart. Intend to connect with your ability to reason. Feel the reasonableness there. Breathe in, and breathe out.

Feel your heart. It's a sensitive area. You can actually sense from your heart. See and sense from your heart. You can imagine eyes on your heart, if you wish.

See the feelings there. Now, let yourself feel the feelings you find there. Feel all the feelings that are to be felt, both in and around the heart area.

Now, locate the box you have built for your emotions. It could be in the center of the chest, or, most likely, to the right. Feel that box. Do you see how you've put emotions there in the past?

Let those emotions come out now. You can turn the box over and let the feelings out.

Feel those feelings.

This is not a thinking exercise right now; it has become a feeling exercise. You can't do it wrong, unless you refuse to feel.

Once you have felt all the feelings that were around the heart and inside the box, you are ready to go on.

Move your consciousness down to your third chakra. See your chakra as bright and yellow, shining.

Notice your consciousness of natural knowing from here. Sense that natural knowing. Make contact with how you just know: you know you know. Allow this sense to permeate your being, to fill your head, to fill your awareness, however it is set to do so.

Now go back to your heart. Can you feel how your heart is happy? It has been acknowledged.

The lesson here is that you can allow yourself to have a feeling life—it's okay. Take time each day to feel your emotions and integrate them into your experience by not having to have the mental involved with everything that you do. Connect to the natural world. Spend time letting emotion have a place in your life. Do things you enjoy and enjoy your time just being. You can use your knowing, but you won't analyze right now. It's important to just be. Allow emotions to color your interactions with others. This will make you a more balanced person and give you a stronger understanding of what you do know. It will bring in the natural knowing more strongly.

By this time, you should be focusing on your natural knowing, still letting that sense penetrate you deeply, shift and change you. Let the knowing affect who you are, where you go from here, and how you are. Let it change and shift your perception. When you leave this meditation, you will be more aware of who you truly are.

Bask in natural knowing for up to five minutes. The goal is to have a brain shift to occur, to train your brain to move to natural knowing when it feels scattered.

This meditation will make you more cohesive and less scattered, and it will allow you to begin to process emotions. This is important, because being scattered and avoiding feelings are yellow traps. The latter can destroy relationships. Also, tendencies to isolate could make it harder to have relationships and for you to feel supported. Specifically, connect to natural knowing and reason in order to see how isolation is a burden, not a path toward fulfillment, and realize that others do not have access to natural knowing like you do. Using reason, recognize that they have their own master chakra gifts as distinct from yours, and teach your gift to them so they can better perceive the world.

# 15

# Green Workbook

### A Spiritual-Spiritual Gift,
### Masculine in Nature: The Natural Fixer

*You might be a green if…*

+ You like the color green.

+ You need to fix things, and you do it constantly
  for everyone you know, not discriminating.

+ You have a critical eye. It's needed to help you
  find balance. You find that without it, you are less
  than yourself. What isn't working out sticks out
  to you like a sore thumb, and you just can't help
  commenting on it.

+ You love nature.

+ You care about larger, world problems, not just your neighborhood's. Still, you are a natural at using minute details, local knowledge, and out-of-the-way awareness to straighten something out. You want to be the doctor that all people want. You tend to work from yourself, outward in concentric rings.

+ You're reasonable (on average).

+ You want to expand slowly, and when possible, to serve more people at the highest levels of awareness.

+ You know how to do things the right way, that there is a right way, and if others used it, they'd get it right (finally). Then you could go home and get some sleep. (You could use some.) You'd wake up the next day and keep going until everything in this life was set up the way it could be for the best interest of all.

+ You have such great accounting skills, you use them to balance all things according to their proper nature of where they should be in space, time, and place.

+ You see how the world works and act according to its ways, either to keep you or others moving in the right direction.

+ You create rules to set in place what works.

+ You must consider options before making what seems to you to be a big decision.

+ You must plan for the contingencies that would come embedded with the outcomes of your decisions, so decisions about how to proceed and how to fix things take awhile.

+ You use your five senses more like an animal does. You use the information they procure as some of your best for finding out what to do next and how to proceed from here. That's why when you set up a process, you expect it to be followed. That comes across in your voice.

+ You see the potential problems coming up ahead and attempt to avert them.

+ You are creative, and you love to build things— whether physically or intangibly.

+ You seek privacy when you work. You like to work from behind the curtain, like the Wizard of Oz in the Emerald City.

+ You dislike the spotlight.

+ Your knowledge is esoteric in nature and other people often don't understand how you got it or where it came from.

+ You can create your own solutions out of thin air, according to others.

+ You don't want to explain to other people how you work or how you figure things out. You will if necessary. It just isn't your first priority. You'll often forget to do it, or it just doesn't seem right.

+ You don't always tell people how to do things just because you know.

+ You can be grumpy—and this goes for any green. You see too much of where the world has gone wrong, in your opinion.

+ You're efficient at using your energy, time, and resources. You don't waste time; you don't waste money.

+ You are not clear about which pieces go where when you are out of balance, and that can scramble your words and your peace of mind.

+ You are not especially good at verbally expressing yourself in times of distress.

+ You always strive for peace of mind and heart.

+ You maintain peace and calm where others freak out.

+ Your favorite thing to say is, "All is well," or a version thereof.

+ You calm things down, smooth things over,
  and straighten things out so they can be clear
  and balanced, not so the problem can resurface
  another day.

+ You drill down to the root of the problem and fix
  it where it started.

+ You see pain as necessary to healing and you
  aren't afraid of it, or afraid to inflict it, because
  you know why it's there; it gives you clues on how
  to move forward and solve the issue.

+ You have a deep, abiding love for other people
  in pain and crisis, wishing and wanting to help
  them. You'll ignore social convention to do so.

+ You feel that you are strong and must stay strong
  for others. When you can't be strong, you don't
  feel like yourself, and that's hard.

+ Other people sometimes envy your abilities to get
  clear and follow your heart, to get the job done
  efficiently and fast, and do it in style. That's just
  your way of doing things; doing them to a high
  standard of living.

+ You are insightful about money and where it
  comes from. You know how to make it. You know
  how to save it when that's important to you.

+ Your friends seek you out for financial advice.

+ You know how much money you have at any given time.

+ You know how to fix things strategically, including people's finances, because those really begin at the heart.

+ You check out your clothes when you are dressed to see that you look good. You are rarely caught not looking your best.

+ You know how to keep things clean and organized for yourself, other people, and the world.

+ You become dejected when you don't honor keeping things clean and organized. A clean house makes for a stable heart and mind.

+ You wish people would stop breaking things and creating messes for you to clean up.

+ You can get exhausted when engaged in resolving major issues over time, but you still approach awareness from the perspective of resolution of all realities into a single formulation for success.

+ You don't understand how the world got to be the way that it did: polluted with twisted belief systems and people out of awareness of what's really going on.

### *When in their giftedness, greens tend to ...*
*(According to Joseph Crane)*

+ Be healers, both physical and spiritual.

+ Be fixers.

+ Be accountants.

+ Be the most balanced of the soul-ray colors; things are or they are not.

+ Be very loyal and compassionate.

+ Be dependable, punctual, and creative.

+ Be willing to give of themselves to others.

+ Teach awareness and divine wisdom.

+ Bring enlightenment and insight.

+ Have mystical knowledge that can heal both the physical and the mystical.

+ Be at peace in the spiritual sense and in touch with their five senses. Through this, they bring the healing of all.

+ Know what is best and how to do it.

+ Be kind and generous and have a deep feeling for others.

+ They want everything to run smoothly and do their best to see that it does.

+ They offer themselves to the greater good of everyone.

## *When in their traps, greens tend to …*
### *(According to Joseph Crane)*

+ Not be fun to be around—they want it all their way and they will put others down to get it.

+ Make other people objects and don't care what they say or do to them.

+ Use people around them as tools only to get the results they want.

+ Believe it is the process that matters, not the person—like the surgeon who operates just to operate, to thrill at the process and how skilled they have become—it matters not if the patient dies.

+ Become cold and calculating, with the ends justifying the means.

+ Do harm so that they can fix it.

+ Know when they're in their traps (the sad part), but won't do anything about it.

+ Pry and get on your nerves.

# Reflection Questions

The following questions will help you explore your gift and how you are using it.

While answering these questions, refer back to the information you just read about the gifts and traps as necessary.

1. You and your soul-ray color are both gifts, and as such, you have gifts to share with the world. This makes you a master, or expert, on how this gift is done. How do you see yourself living in your gifts?

2. Which aspects of your gift seem new to you? (Maybe you've never thought about them before.)

3. Which aspects of your gift would you like to embrace more fully now that you are consciously aware that you have special access to them? What would be the result?

4. What traps do you currently struggle with in your life? Traps are not "bad," however, they may feel inconvenient or unpleasant. When they occur, you are turned toward the darkness, rather than the light.

5. Can you identify triggers that move you into your traps?

6. The way out of a trap for a green is to "give themselves the gifts they give to others," and give out of nothing but the love of God. How would your life change if you did this often?

7. There is a meditation at the end of this workbook to assist you in giving yourself your own gift. I encourage you to think of your own methods to help you connect with giving from God. Which ones can you think of right now?

8. Can you set a goal to become good at recognizing when you are in your gifts, and when you are in your traps? How long do you think it would take? Which do you want to accomplish first?

9. What questions do you have about your gift?

10. Do you have any insights about what it is like to have this gift? No one knows your gift like you! Please share your insights below.

11. Sometimes greens become overwhelmed with the amount that needs to be balanced and fixed. Because you see so many things that need balancing and fixing, even as these things are not anticipated by the rest of the population and are constantly escaping their notice, there can be a tendency to become disillusioned. Remembering the perfection in the imperfection can help with this. In fact, such remembrance can help a green balance their desire to fix things in all areas of their life and move forward to do what they can right now. How do you know if something is perfect? Good enough?

12. Write about how you see perfection in imperfection: what is perfect about your most irritating mess right now? How does it feel when you say, "bless this mess"?

13. Remembering that there is no good, bad, right, or wrong, that there just "is," take some time to think back on all the times when you may have seen something that needed to be fixed but never fixed it. What were the results?

14. Once a problem has been identified, you yearn to fix it; you desire to find the specific solution that will work best. You will then tend to explore the options—waiting and looking for just the right solution—get into the details, and really look to see what will help. Only then, when you are sure of a solution, do you move forward. This is a strength, to be sure. Describe a time when you used this kind of thoroughness to fix a problem, to find a way to fix it once and for all.

15. Greens are sometimes on a roll with finding the next, the next, and then the next thing that is wrong—and pointing it out—to where it exhausts their listener. This harkens back to the trap of wanting to fix things that are not necessarily in need of being fixed What do you think you could do about monitoring your rate of finding problems in the world and expressing them?

16. What I find can help in this regard is Archangel Michael's recommendation that everyone do things

out of emotion instead of out of a sense of obligation, so we stay awake.

Greens can check to see whether what they are doing comes from emotion or not. You can do things just from emotion to regulate how much you fix—and the prospect of even thinking about this will help you to determine how much it's possible to fix. You want to find ways to align with doing things out of the love of God.

Write about how you feel about doing things from the perspective of emotion.

17. Sometimes, you want to control the process and make sure things get done the way you see they should be. If you use someone as though they were a tool, will that help you stay in your gift? How can you involve people in your procedure and also let people have sovereignty over themselves?

18. Greens are good at setting boundaries. Can you think of a time when you did a great job at this? Is this an ability you can explore or expand? How so?

19. Sometimes greens can come across to others as being too strong or critical. Do you feel you need to make any modifications in this area? How would you go about doing that if needed? (It is possible to share the light of your gift in ways that others can hear and receive. You can be true to yourself yet also understand how you might remember communication tools in doing so.)

20. Sometimes, it can be hard to receive from others the things we do for them so well—strength, and bringing things into balance. Write about how you can be more conscious, aware, and receptive to receiving your gift from others, either from another green or someone else. How would this help you? How would it change you?

21. Greens often do well when they have yellow friends. (See the appendix for a description of all the spiritual gifts.) The yellow spiritual gift is the gift of the natural thinker and knower. Yellows help greens feel expanded. One reason for this is because greens have a need to transcend the black and white thinking that occurs with their gift. They desire to either know that something is or is not, but the lack of patience that this sometimes engenders can be hard. Yellows can show a wider, broader path and get you thinking differently. They can clean up your thought process and help you be more broad-minded, or not see in black and white, but see higher truths at work. Do you know any yellows? How can you tell? What are the telling characteristics?

22. Describe what you have noticed about what it's like to interact with yellows. In your own words and experience, what do they do for you? What can you do for them?

23. Now, review the observations about how yellows and greens need each other in the Light Partners chapter.

Greens and yellows don't just make good chakra friends, they also make ideal romantic partners. If you were in a position to experience this, how could it help you in your lifestyle?

24. Because of the complementary nature of the yellow and green energies, greens and yellows could really use their compliment sometimes. Do you have a yellow friend who cares for you? If not, can you be on the lookout for one?

25. How do you feel about being green? What it is like? What do you like the best about it? If you were to describe your gift to someone else, and let them know what it is like, what would you say?

26. Go to YouTube and listen to Kermit the Frog's "It's Not Easy Being Green." What do you make of this song? How does it relate to you?

27. Greens are good at effecting a profound and complete change on a person's life. Can you remember a time when you did this recently?

28. Greens aren't afraid to go back again and again to get it right. They will hang in there. Can you think of a time when you did likewise? How do you think that strengthens you and makes you an asset to others?

29. Honoring your gift is very important. The more you honor it in yourself, the more others will honor it in you and the less likely you are to be walked on or your gifts disregarded. You will gain more respect for who you are and your light will shine brighter because these things will be present in you. In fact, they already are in a much deeper way simply because you've engaged this much with this information so far. What commitment are you willing to make regarding honoring yourself in the future?

30. How can you honor yourself for your own greatness?

31. Envision by drawing or writing what it means to be a green and what you will accomplish in the future with your gifts.

## Daily Practices

The following sequence of questions will help you notice your gifts more and how you share them. It will help you grow in your light, the light of who you are, and avoid pitfalls you may have or be experiencing on a large scale. You can continue these practices as long as you wish as a helpful check and to raise awareness about living in giftedness, your special way of living in the light. The more aware you are, the more you will be able to avoid your traps and their associated consequences.

*Reflection on your soul-ray color:*

1. In what ways did you live out of your gift today? Be specific. Please refer to the description of your gift and its traps when completing this section.

2. Did you catch yourself going into any traps today? Were you able to avoid these traps?

3. Are you in a trap now and not aware of it? If so, what would you like to do about it? Make a decision and a commitment now. Either give yourself your gift right here and now, or make a decision to take action in this regard tomorrow.

4. To stay clear, consider memorizing your gifts and traps and striving to apply the solutions for getting out of your traps once you're in them.

The following list is a reminder of how to exit from your traps. Because greens can shade yellow and blue once in a while, you will get stuck in these two colors' traps. If you suspect this is happening, you may use the list to remember how to remove yourself from the trap of these other colors as well.

*List of exits from green's traps ...*

+ Use your intuition to tell you what is needed in a situation where you don't feel at your best.

+ Ask yourself what you need right now.

- Connect to your natural knowing and ability to reason (yellow).

- Give out of nothing except for the love of God (green).

- Give yourself love and wisdom (blue).

## More Aspects of Your Gift

Now, let's talk more about that aspect of being a green, which is that greens can shade blue and yellow in order to live out their gifts. Reflect now on how, why, or when you shade blue and yellow, the chakras on either side of your master chakra. Read the description of blues in their giftedness and then answer the questions below.

1. When do you most often find yourself utilizing blue?

2. Could you expand this ability to serve a purpose?

While no one is a yellow like a yellow, greens can prove very familiar with yellow by close proximity (the solar plexus and the heart chakras are right next to each other.) Read the description of yellows in their giftedness and then answer the questions below.

1. When do you most often find yourself utilizing yellow?

2. Could you expand this ability, to serve a purpose?

## Meditation to Bring One Into Giving Out of Nothing Except for the Love of God

The following meditation will assist you in exiting from any of the green traps.

> Sit with your feet flat on the floor, with palms facing up on your lap.

> Visualize a ball of grace (God's love) at the top of your head.

> Breathe in grace, resting it on your heart. Exhale anything that is bothering you or concerning you.

> Breathe in grace, resting it on your heart, letting it permeate your heart chakra and heart.

> Breathe in grace one more time, exhaling any stuck emotions.

> Imagine your crown chakra opening up like a flower.

> Imagine an infinity symbol.

> Make this infinity symbol as large as you can.

> Draw it huge and blue in the sky of the universe.

> Imagine an image of yourself standing on the earth in a beautiful natural environment:

> It's summer—the green grass is growing and the green trees are waving.

Now, imagine a green and pink infinity symbol large enough for you to stand on. Place it beneath your feet.

Jump on this symbol.

If you fall off, jump back on.

Jump up and down on this symbol. Do this several times.

Stop, and integrate the energies flowing into your system. You will see this symbol connect with your energy and body. You are in the middle of this symbol, and it's running its energy into you just like an IV.

Stay here for as long as needed.

Once the entire infinity symbol has been absorbed, it is empty. Let what is left disintegrate.

Bring in all the energy you need from the entire universe. Imagine it all coming to you now.

Now, visualize yourself giving to others. Give all the things that you love and want to give to others in the future, and imagine it now.

See it in a movie, real-time, but it's the real future. Your future.

Source the love deep within your heart. You see yourself with a heart growing out of your heart—there is a heart coming out of your heart and it can be given from and to others.

Give from this space.

You are now there. You are in a space where you can give out of nothing but the love of God.

You are in your gifts.

Carry this vibration with you when you give and receive.

Bless your heart with kindness and compassion.

Whenever you bring in the infinity symbol and give from the love of God, you're assisting yourself in stepping into the light and out of the darkness of your trap.

You can jump back on the infinity symbol throughout your day as needed.

## All's Well That Ends Well

Things start to move when resistance disappears. It seems like once someone decides to do something one way, because they can't do it another, then they let go of the problem that had arisen through resistance, and the way for the original choice opens up. That's always happening in the green world: deciding to do one thing then doing the opposite instead. Because you're in charge of releasing the resistance the rest of us have to healing and growing, you go back over things not only consciously, but unconsciously—helping other people return to wholeness.

It may seem like you are circling back toward old ground, but that ground is now on a higher plane. Can you think of more ways to complete the healing process on anything outstanding for you?

# 16

# Blue Workbook

## A Spiritual-Mental Gift, Masculine in Nature: The Natural Teacher

*You might be a blue if . . .*

+ You have been called a patient teacher and friend.

+ You are honest, upright, and people can count on you. You're true blue.

+ You relate to people through your mental body, but need love to feel you're at your best and make your teachings sound. Love lights the way.

+ You are passionate about sharing what you know with others, so that they can be their best (and avoid trouble).

+ You're sitting around somewhere and suddenly you think of something you have to tell a specific person.

+ You teach about yourself not out of ego but because who you are and how you operate is instructive to others.

+ You talk about yourself a lot, eager to share what you have to say.

+ You talk a lot, in general.

+ You understand that actions have consequences and will often predict the consequences of actions for yourself and others.

+ You have a desire to give to others, whatever they need.

+ You frequently give away facts, information (knowledge), advice (wisdom), books, philosophies, music, or anything that you think would have special meaning to that person.

+ You are the best at coming up with opinions that alienate people from their self-inflicted wounds.

+ The idea of not having to answer a question seems strange, because you relish answering questions and will usually answer them, even when they are embarrassing.

+ You speak in contraries to show points of view. You say things like, "e-mail is so important, but it's a drag," and "this is the best place to live, but really it isn't fit for anyone to live here."

+ In class, you will answer other students' questions when the teacher is not answering them. By the same token, you will answer the teacher's questions when no one is answering them.

+ You can become a teacher even if you are not trained in that direction.

+ Your knowledge comes from places you can't always explain to others.

+ You share a sense of solidarity with others, and always look for that, or want to create it if it isn't there.

+ You are willing to offend others by giving them unwanted opinions to keep them safe from harm.

+ You know when someone is being treated worse than someone else—and you advocate change to rectify the situation.

+ You work all the time to make sure that all have a fair shot.

+ You can get angry when things aren't fair and you can't see a way to make them right.

- You will go out of your way to help people or groups that you feel were left behind, have gotten less, or just deserve it.

- You need mental stimulation and smart people around you.

- You see the intelligence in people others consider to be less-than.

- You like diversity.

- You see the positive inside the negative. You think negative experiences complete the circle of life.

- You have to get out of the house on a regular basis to run, bike, walk, dance, or whatever is your preference.

- You find yourself talking about spiritual topics anytime, anyplace, anywhere.

- No one can censor you, silence you, or feed you their words.

- You will go to great lengths to find and give other people the information they need.

### When in their giftedness, blues tend to...
(*According to Joseph Crane*)

- Be teachers.

- Be keepers of the gates of wisdom.

+ Let in the light of knowledge.

+ Have this loftiness.

+ Bring you knowledge.

+ Be one of giving—their love is impersonal.

+ Be one with Christ Consciousness.

+ Be perfectly balanced in male and female and the most balanced in body, emotions, mind and spirit.

+ Bring out the best in people.

+ Care that you become the best you can be, and be relentless about it.

## When in their traps, blues tend to ...
*(According to Joseph Crane)*

+ Teach you that you will never arrive—you'll never get enough information to know as much as they do.

+ Be drama queens.

+ Become unbalanced.

+ Become unapproachable, haughty.

+ Appear pompous, arrogant, and self-centered.

+ Claim you are stupid, while they know it all.

+ Apologize and eat humble pie.

+ Talk too much.

## Reflection Questions

While answering these questions, refer back to the information you just read about the gifts and traps as necessary.

1. You and your soul-ray color are both gifts, and as such, you have gifts to share with the world. This makes you a master, or expert, on how this gift is done. How do you see yourself living in your gifts?

2. Which aspects of your gift seem new to you? (Maybe you've never thought about them before.)

3. Which aspects of your gift would you like to embrace more fully, now that you are consciously aware that you have special access to them? What would be the result?

4. What traps do you currently struggle with in your life? Traps are not "bad," however, they may feel inconvenient or unpleasant. Traps occur when you are not turned toward the light.

5. Can you identify triggers that move you into your traps?

6. Can you set a goal to become good at recognizing when you are in your gifts, and when you are in your traps? How long do you think it would take? Which do you want to accomplish first?

7. What questions do you have about your gift?

8. Do you have any insights about what it is like to have this gift? No one knows your gift like you! Please share your insights below.

9. To you, what does it mean to teach?

10. Speech, or communication, is very important to a blue. After all, the blue gift comes through the throat chakra; in order to teach, one must communicate, and communication is the primary means by which blues teach. Teaching can also be done in other ways, yet verbal skills are always readily at hand in any situation, and that makes talking the most versatile teaching method. Describe how you may have found yourself— on an impromptu basis—teaching either friends or strangers in the past.

11. Who is a teacher? Our conventional view of teachers is that they must go to school to obtain a certificate and be taught to teach. Yet blues are the natural teachers— when they are shown how to teach, they will still resort to their own strategies of speaking off the cuff, not needing materials to be pre-prepared. They were born with a few tricks up their sleeves. They have innate ability they've developed on their own. How do you teach?

Put a blue in front of a classroom of willing students, and without a teaching certificate, they will do just fine. Do they know everything about how to reach every misbehaved child with certain information with the institutional settings in our public schools? Maybe not without specific training in classroom management and reading strategies—but that is not the way we are talking about teaching right now.

My position is that the blue spiritual gift defines teaching, not that the teaching field defines teaching itself. Look to the blue spiritual gift to see what it is teaching is all about. We're talking about enlightenment here.

Institutions do have a lot to offer us as teachers, yet the bodies of knowledge in these places was constructed by both blues and non-blues, and various motivations come into play when you have a view of teaching that has been put together by people of all the gifts (since so many different people of different soul-ray colors want to be teachers for a career.)

12. Can you embrace yourself as a teacher in spite of the fact that you may not have a formal teaching degree? How would that change your attitude about how you approach others? What would that do for your confidence and self-expression?

13. What if you thought about all the communication you did as teaching? What if you stopped thinking of it as just talking and started honoring the many-layered messages instead? How would that change you and what you have to share?

14. People everywhere are in need of wisdom for their life. You receive messages from the divine and are

prompted by your own internal leanings to share them. You have been spending a lot of time collecting information, truth, and wisdom to share through the books you read and observations you make, too.

You are good at perceiving what others need to hear in any situation. Though it can feel like it, nothing random is going on. You are in the right place at the right time. Perfectly positioned to see into that person, and receiving of the knowledge you need to give them. The only question is, will you teach—will you share what you know? Or will you hold back? God put you there.

Because you sometimes experience a sense of stage fright with regard to interacting with others on the basis of cosmic knowledge, take some time to consider when you may have held back your gift. You can see, based on past experience, how the knowledge you share will impact a person's life. Haven't you seen what happens when you *don't* share the message? What could people be missing out on?

15. Now, let's look at what happens when you *do* live in your gift wholeheartedly. When the teacher teaches, she is in her gift. When she will not teach, she's in a trap. Write about some of the times when you enlightened someone about what was going on in their life, or life in general, and it made a big impact. Did that person thank you later? What did they experience? Do you see how you brought in the light?

16. Now that you've thought about what happens when your teaching does and does not happen, how would you like to adjust when and how much you talk, teach, or enlighten others? What kind of commitment are you willing to make when prompted?

17. Did anyone ever tell you that you were not a good communicator? Or that you were not a good teacher? How did that make you feel? Do you still carry either belief? Write down the belief you would like to hold and how you can act to practice it every day until it becomes something that you deeply know.

   *Examples:*

   I am a great communicator.

   I am a good teacher.

   Come up with your own variations of these beliefs below.

   New Core Belief 1: _____

   New Core Belief 2: _____

   New Core Belief 3: _____

   List ways you will take action to help integrate your new beliefs

18. Blues would do well to be open to going anywhere and doing anything in service of their teaching gift—not limiting themselves to where and when they would

teach. They can teach about topics they know a lot and a little about. This is because they are constantly being given (and looking into) more information about what is happening. What would happen if you were more open to teaching in different situations? Can you think of jobs or projects you might take on? Settings where you might speak up?

19. It's good for you as a blue to "let the wild horses run," or let your energy go where it needs to go. How can this metaphor help you on your journey? What does it feel like when you contemplate doing that? How does that spiritually refresh you?

20. Sometimes blues talk too much in their traps. Can you think of times when you have done this? Write about that here. My definition of talking too much is when you've held the floor far longer than anyone else and eyes are glazing over. What are the signals that let you know when you've been talking too much? (They may be internal or external. You may hear words, get a feeling or a knowing, or make some observation.)

21. If you notice you've been talking too much, what can you do?

22. When blues are in their traps, they might get angry or resentful. This is because the teacher can see what is going on, but not everyone else does. When other

people don't see how consequences fit with actions, sometimes it makes them behave in an immature manner. You tend to assume that others have your knowledge. But they don't. That's why they have you. Take a moment to reflect on how you can use your awareness to be a resource rather than feel put out when people confuse you. Have you noticed yourself feeling bitter when you focus on other people's actions and how they could have improved? How can you take responsibility for yourself in those situations?

23. When you've done your gift from God and shared what it is you wanted to share, can you let go of the outcome? Is it possible to passionately deliver what people need without needing to control their behavior?

24. Every teacher needs someone to teach and something to teach. There is a difference between teaching a single person at a time and teaching a group. Let's take a look at how each situation brings out your gifts. Compare how you feel when you are enlightening one person versus when you are working with a group. Where does more power occur? Does it change what you say and how you say it? Can you see yourself shining in your light during these times?

25. Blues are great at speaking in front of people. Even if you feel apprehensive about it, you were built to speak to large crowds of people, five hundred or more at

a time! Have you ever noticed yourself in your own intensity around others, talking in a loud voice? That's the blue that wants to come out and teach the group. Do you have stage fright? If so, can you think of or research ways to move past it?

26. What teachings could you give in a group setting that would be different than those you could accomplish one-on-one? Who could you reach? With what message or messages?

27. What do you most like to talk about? One big source of your teachings is yourself, your own life, and your experiences. When you talk about yourself, what do you usually learn? Most of us have favorite topics and themes. What is one theme you'd like to study in order to be able to learn, and then share more about it?

28. When a person has enthusiasm and natural, projective voicing, it's important to intentionally develop a one-on-one way of relating to people. If you find you blow people away with your intensity, write below about how you'd like to be one-on-one. The first step is creating a goal for yourself.

29. Blue energy loves to expand. This means you can create a lot, very quickly. Sometimes, when this process of expansion is over or at rest before the next expansion, it can leave you feeling lonely or like you are not

enough. Not feeling like you are enough is another blue trap. Imagine what integrating the belief that "I am enough" would do for your life.

Blues engage others with general speech. They are smart. Listening to the divine and working with others at the same time requires you to be more esoteric when you speak. Sometimes blues can be judged for the language they use and even told not to use it.

Then again, there can also be times when a blue falls into the trap of being aloof and arrogant. This is getting into a habit of knowing it all and lording it over other people, however subtly: you know it when you do it. This is the ego at work, which takes things in relation only to the self; it's you making the words about yourself instead of about the other person, as a means of transactional understanding.

30. I'd like to invite you to think about both scenarios. Where did you see that you were judged for using language that is just second nature to you? You used the words that you needed to for the time:

31. Have you ever held yourself superior to others in your language and bearing, or were so high in the stratosphere they couldn't understand you?

32. To stay at their best and to live in the light, blues must be balanced. When you do something to balance the overall mental, emotional, physical, and spiritual parts

of yourself and bring them into sync, you will be living in your light. The four bodies are like the legs of a table. When one leg is shorter than another, you can't function well. Visualize them. Which one seems compromised right now, if any? What can you do about it? If you found that one of them was out of balance and it's been weeks or more since it became that way, can you create a long-term strategy to bring yourself to alignment?

Visualize those four legs of a table: body, mind, emotion, and spirit. Which one seems compromised right now (if any)? What can you do about it?

33. A blue needs to have a spiritual, mental, emotional, and physical experience each day to stay balanced. If a blue spends most of his or her day in mental activities, such as for work, then the rest of the day should be more focused on the other types of explorations or activities. Describe how your life and schedule must change in order to accommodate this new information.

34. My ultimate advice for standing in the light of who you are as a blue is to keep your physical, emotional, mental, and spiritual balance, and violate it for the sake of no one. This means no matter what friend, boss, or program leader asks you to go out of balance, you don't, for you know that balance is your everything. Obviously it's a process and sometimes we'll drop the

ball. The point here is for you to stay strong in your commitment to yourself to live in your own light.

To compare to other gifts—if an orange gets out of balance, it isn't going to affect the giving of that gift in the way that a blue will be affected by the same. What works for other colors doesn't necessarily work for blues. So take time to write down activities that keep you moving in each of the following areas. I've included some examples just to get you started.

### Activities That Feed Me and Keep Me Whole

| Physical | Mental | Emotional | Spiritual |
|---|---|---|---|
| Eating. My preferred exercise. | Reading. Conversing with friends and family on topics of interest to them (this gives you an opportunity to teach). | Hanging out with friends or significant other face-to-face and sharing emotions when you relate. Feeling and dialoguing emotions to see where they are coming from and what they tell you. | Engaging in a spiritual practice or process. Reading a spiritual book. |

35. How do others handle your wisdom? Do you believe they recognize it as such? How could you help them listen even better?

36. As a blue, you have certain core teachings that you tend to share. What are some of them?

37. The way out of a trap, for a blue, is to give yourself the gifts you give to others—love and wisdom. Holding onto the power of love, according to Archangel Michael, can make every other emotion take a step back. How would your life change if you brought more love into it? There is a meditation at the end of this workbook to assist you in giving yourself love and wisdom. I invite you to try it and see what happens.

38. Blues are great at communicating but not always so great at listening. The gift puts the blue above the conversation; however, it's important to be able to receive in addition to give. How could you become a better listener?

Sometimes you get on a roll. You might lecture. And some people need that. But sometimes we also need to have a conversation. Try this exercise: Practice saying something to get a response. Then be quiet, and let the person respond. Repeat. Only say things to connect and get responses. This will give you an idea of what it's like to be in the conversation rather than above it.

39. How will you balance lecturing and conversing in the future?

40. Blues will often want to hear information from another blue to verify its veracity. Can you think of other blues in your life who you have gone to for information, mentorship, or understanding? Every blue needs other blues in his or her life, because blues understand blues on their own terms. Any color does. List your blue friends here along with their strengths.

There is another soul-ray color that blues are very in tune with. Purples are blue's official reciprocal color because they remind us of the importance of love. This is important because blues focus so much with their mental faculties. In addition to this, purples have an innate respect for the teacher archetype and do seek to be taught.

41. Read about the purple spiritual gift in the appendix and reflect on any thoughts you have about that gift here.

42. Do you know any purples? How can you tell?

43. Talk about what it's like to interact with purples. What do they do for you? What can you do for them from your perspective?

44. Now, review how blues and purples benefit from each other's company in the Reciprocal Chakras section of the Light Partners chapter. People of the purple and

blue master chakras make good friends and colleagues and also ideal romantic partners due to this dynamic. What are some insights you have about this? How could being in a relationship with a purple affect the way you live your life?

45. Your answer is perfect for you. What energies or patterns would need to change in order for you to attract a person with a purple master chakra?

46. How do you feel about being blue? What is it like? What do you like the best about it? The least about it? If you were to describe your gift to someone else, and let them know what it is like, what would you say?

47. Honoring your gift is very important. The more you honor it in yourself, the more others will honor it in you. The less likely you are to be walked on or your gifts disregarded. You will gain more respect for who you are and your light will shine more brightly because these things will be present in you. In fact, they already are in a much deeper way, simply because you've engaged this much with this information so far. What commitment are you willing to make regarding honoring yourself in the future?

48. How can you honor yourself for your own greatness?

49. Envision by drawing or writing what it means to be a blue and what you will accomplish in the future with your gifts.

## Daily Practices

The following sequence of questions will help you notice your gifts more and how you share them. It will help you grow in your light, the light of who you are, and avoid pitfalls you may have or be experiencing on a large scale. You can continue these practices for as long as you wish, to check your awareness about how much you live in gifted states of being. The more aware you are, the more you will be able to avoid your traps and their associated consequences.

*Reflection on your soul-ray color:*

1. In what ways did you live out of your gift today? Be specific. Please refer to the overview of the soul-ray colors in the appendix when completing this section.

2. Did you catch yourself going into any traps today? Were you able to avoid these traps?

3. Are you in a trap now and not aware of it? If so, what would you like to do about it? Make a decision and a commitment now. Either give yourself your gift right here and now, or make a decision to take action in this regard tomorrow.

4. Simply coming into awareness of your gifts and traps is a large feat in the beginning. Consider memorizing your gifts and traps in order to be able to know the nuances and when you must shift from one to the other.

The following list is a reminder of how to exit from the blue trap. Because blues can shade green or purple once in a while, blues can be in a trap of either of these two colors. If you suspect this is happening, you may use the following list to remember how to remove yourself from the trap of the other color.

*List of exits from blue's traps ...*

+ Use your intuition to tell you what is needed in a situation where you don't feel at your best.

+ Ask yourself what you need right now.

+ Know that the power you have comes from the love of God (green).

+ Give yourself wisdom and love (blue).

+ Know that God will give you everything you need, materially (purple).

## More Aspects of Your Gift

Now, let's talk more about that aspect of being a blue, which is that blues can shade green and purple in order to become who they shall be. Reflect now on how, why, or when you shade green and purple, the chakras on either side of your master chakra. Read the description of greens in their giftedness and then answer the questions below.

1. When do you most often find yourself utilizing green?

2. Could you expand this ability to serve a purpose?

While no one can be a purple like a purple, blues can prove very familiar with this territory because it's right next to them on the chakra system. Your teaching can be more creative when you visit your purple chakra and integrate its gifts. Read the description of purples in their giftedness and then answer the questions below.

1. When do you most often find yourself being purple?

2. Could you increase this ability to serve a purpose?

## Meditation to Bring in Love and Wisdom

This is a meditation to assist you in exiting from the blue traps. When you are in a trap, you can do this meditation to bring yourself into the light.

Imagine a column of white light coming down from the heavens and through the top of your head, and meeting at your heart.

Connect with your guides and angels. Say, "I consciously connect with my guides and angels now and ask them to assist me in this process."

Feel the love you have in your own heart, for yourself. Feel the love your angels and guides are giving you.

Imagine a ball of grace (God's love) at your crown chakra; begin to breathe in that grace, and rest it on your heart.

Put out your hands. With your right hand, invite wisdom. See wisdom as an image or form of a person, place, or thing, and put that image in your right hand. Stay with it for a moment.

Bring your right hand to rest on your heart, absorbing this wisdom into your being, letting it become one with you.

Now, put out your left hand. Imagine a red heart of love in your hand. Bring as much love to your hand as possible. Place your left hand over your right hand on your heart. Allow this love, of all that is, to permeate your being.

Now see a heart, with the word "wisdom" written over it, move to your high heart (upper left shoulder). This connects you with divine love. Breathe in divine love and grace.

Continue to merge, with intention, with the love and wisdom. Do this until you have the answers you were looking for regarding any situation that was troubling you.

Take this love and wisdom into the world, and do whatever you wish with it.

This meditation can be done until it feels automatic and repeated if you feel out of balance. You can learn to connect with your love and wisdom any time.

Connect with love and wisdom each time you feel yourself out of balance emotionally, spiritually, physically, or mentally. Give this gift (which you give to others) to yourself. It points you toward the light and releases you from the bondage of your traps.

# 17

# Purple Workbook

## A Spiritual-Emotional Spiritual Gift, Masculine in Nature: The Natural Artist

*You might be a purple if ...*

+ People always tell you their stories. When you come around, they just start talking and they tell you everything.

+ You can listen to someone's most self-incriminating story and make them feel better without saying a word. Your presence and energy alone does the trick.

+ You help others release emotional baggage by listening to them, making it okay that they have their emotional reactions, and learning to love them anyway.

+ You turn people's worst nightmares into things they can easily get over. Your love lets them do that. All you need is love. All they need is care.

+ Your insights make things better between people.

+ You create opportunities for people to come together in love and trust.

+ You feel good after you help someone in emotional distress and destruction.

+ You'll show up when there is emotional distress and quite as mysteriously go elsewhere when you're no longer needed.

+ You give your presence as a gift from God.

+ You inject softness into interpersonal relationships and make them go more smoothly; your input helps relationships happen in loving ways.

+ You're the best at keeping a relationship together, and you won't give up on the other person. You won't stop loving that person even if they leave you or you do decide to part ways.

+ Things flow much better in your life when you have a romantic relationship and you know this is true because you tend to become more chaotic and disjointed without one (for adults).

+ You love romance.

+ You can shepherd a relationship through the darkest of times, when everyone else would have given up.

+ You see sex as another expression of humankind's care for each other.

+ You love the opposite sex. You are good with them.

+ You move with the ebbs and flows of relationships with an intimate understanding of them.

+ You make the other person feel like they deserve the best when they are with you.

+ It's easy to create something. Your imagination often shows up in the real world as something that really occurs in your life—kind of like a movie.

+ You always want to stay connected.

+ You wish you never had to end a relationship, though you know it's necessary.

+ You have complaints, and you won't hold them back after a certain point.

+ You have the ability to get very angry or be in another dark mood for some time then snap out of it smiling like nothing ever happened.

+ You are quick to smile and quicker to frown when down. But you know people have to get it out. If people fight around you, you can almost stand it.

+ If someone doesn't behave in a loving way toward you, that's the worst that can happen.

+ You abhor abrasion.

+ You love people and you give to them more than they give to you.

+ You are always giving your time, your space, and your energy to others.

+ You always wanted to make things as a child.

+ You are tempted to make something that you see multiple times a day.

+ You make things so you don't have to buy them, either to save money or because what you saw in the store isn't enough.

+ You see making things as better than buying them.

+ You work harder on what is important to you than most people. You do it to put love into it.

+ You succeed when the work is done and it's the most important masterpiece of your lifetime, a life achievement. That's what you're going for, and you'll stop at nothing to make it your own creation, your personal making by your signature.

+ You have your own aesthetic. You know what looks good, and you do things up to your own standards.

+ You have your own ability to flow with space, light, and time. You are naturally kinesthetic in the areas of physicality, preferring day jobs that allow you to move, such as acting, occupational therapy, photography, or farming (not desk jobs).

## When in their giftedness, purples tend to ...
*(According to Joseph Crane)*

+ Be creative people.

+ Show up in advertising.

+ Be artists, sculptors, musicians, writers, actors, poets, and dancers.

+ Become priests or spiritual teachers in the art of creation.

+ Teach divine love, expressed through that which they create—love, science, music, and art.

+ Embrace contemplation and sincerity, which brings forth justice in the work they do.

+ Bring the gift of creativity to the world.

*When in their traps, purples tend to ...*
*(According to Joseph Crane)*

+ Make it all about personal glory, personal riches, money, and fame.

+ Become obsessed with materialism; it can be about the project instead of themselves, but they must have the best of everything—they won't "make do."

+ Become full of themselves and their self-importance.

+ Really think they have arrived; whatever they do is for themselves.

+ Do third rate work, using second rate mediums, with ideas borrowed from others.

+ Lose the ability to create and yet still demand first-rate prices.

+ Sell their gift of creation, which becomes evident in their work.

## Reflection Questions

The following questions will help you explore your gift, its traps, and how to be better about them and yourself. While answering these questions, refer back to the information you just read about the gifts and traps as necessary.

1. You and your soul-ray color are both gifts, and as such, you have gifts to share with the world. This makes you a master, or expert, on how this gift is done. How do you see yourself living in your gifts?

2. Which aspects of your gift seem new to you? (Maybe you've never thought about them before.)

3. Which aspects of your gift would you like to embrace more fully now that you are consciously aware that you have special access to them? What would be the result?

4. What traps do you currently struggle with in your life? Traps are not "bad," however, they may feel inconvenient or unpleasant. Traps occur when you are not turned toward the light.

5. Can you identify triggers that move you into your traps?

6. The way out of your trap is to give yourself the gifts you give to others—divine, nonjudgmental love; power to create; teachings of love; and especially the knowing that God will provide everything that you need. How would your life change if you did this often? There is a meditation at the end of this workbook to help you develop this awareness.

7. Can you set a goal to become good at recognizing when you are in your gifts, and when you are in your traps? How long do you think it would take? Which do you want to accomplish first?

8. What questions do you have about your gift?

9. Do you have any insights about what it is like to have this gift? No one knows your gift like you! Please share your insights below.

10. Purples can have the habit of really needing something to be perfect. Because they spend a lot of time on their art in order to perfect it, this can bleed over into other areas of life (because all of life is art). Some purples need to be perfect with their home, food plan or diet, the lineup of coworkers in the office, and some need to find a relationship with a perfect partner (because of their gift, not because they are a perfectionist). Can you think of something that, either now or in the past, you needed to have perfect? Can you think of and reflect on ways to be more satisfied with what you do see?

11. What art form are you drawn to most at this time? Remember to think outside the box. Some art forms I have seen purples doing are hairdressing, cooking, home decorating, woodworking, gun making, singing, and the list goes on. What form of art do you truly feel drawn to? Stretch yourself! Describe it here or brainstorm a list.

12. What would happen if you started engaging your chosen art form on a daily, or even weekly, basis? How would your life change? How would you feel about yourself?

13. Some purples are drawn more to science than art. This balances the right brain (purple focus) with the left. If you like science, reflect on why.

14. Purples are good at helping others when they are going through emotional pain, drama, and ups and downs. Many purples tell me that people naturally come up to them and tell them about their personal problems (even if they are not dramatic). Can you describe a time when you recently helped someone in this situation?

15. An artist is able to see and express from many perspectives, but in their traps, they see only from one perspective—their own. Have you ever felt narrowed in this way? Some purples are told by friends and family that they are self-centered, which may point out that a trap is in play. How do you suppose you can remedy this?

16. Purples like to be seen. Some purples will make a big deal when they come into a room so that everyone looks at them. Purples, of course, many times have a honed sense of fashion. They want to dress themselves in a way that shows style. Comment on your desire to be seen (it's neither good, bad, right nor wrong).

17. Comment on your sense of style, fashion, or how things should look (a row of carrots in the ground, or a painting). What is required?

18. Do you feel that you give to others but they do not give back to you? Why do you suppose this is so? What can you do to manifest different kinds of relationships?

19. Purples do not like pressure. They can also have a hard time committing to a course of action, or committing in general. Depending on the situation, this can be appropriate or it can be detrimental. It depends. What is your relationship with commitment? Are there areas where you could commit more? Less?

20. Archangel Michael advises everyone to do things "out of emotion" not just because we have to; otherwise, we are asleep. My feeling is that this is one of the reasons purples are best at creating things—because they already live in an emotional world and are more likely to automatically do things out of emotion. Comment on your process of creation. How do you go about creating things in your life?

21. Purples are said to like chaos, but that shows up different for different people. Some purples are just okay with a lot of action going on around them. Some actually live in a world of chaos and "live" the chaos. You don't have to live the chaos, you can use it to create what you really want; use your comfort with it to love other people and bring your nascent creations into being. Comment on your relationship with chaos and how you want it to shift.

22. Which traps did you used to fall into that you don't anymore? Where are you still tripping up? Materialism? Having to have the best of everything (people and things)? Self-centeredness?

23. Purples, because of their ability to give love to others, can make people fall in love with them more easily than other colors. Comment on your relationship with yourself in this regard and how you'd like to see it evolve.

24. Purples can go into different aspects of themselves, sometimes aspects of people who they really aren't. They might do this just because they enjoy it. Where are you at on this continuum? Are you pretty real? Or are you a role player? Where does it feel best to be right now? (No right or wrong.) Who do you want to be?

25. Purples are good at becoming chameleons themselves to fit in with different groups and individuals. In doing so, they may lose sight of themselves. Playing a different role can obscure others' perception of your true self and actually keep them from knowing the beautiful you— who you truly are. If you were to get in touch with what you really wanted and who you really were, do you think your friends would change? Why or why not?

26. Purples are said to be complex people. I've never heard a purple say, "I'm a simple man/woman." What kind of people do you like to be around?

27. Of all the seven spiritual gifts, blues, purples, and violets are the most desirous of a primary romantic relationship because they are more stabilized by one than the other colors. Purples usually want to have a primary romantic relationship and often are good at getting into one. Whether this describes you or not, I invite you to be in touch with your true desire in a relationship at this time. Write here what your truest, deepest desire is. Go to your heart and ask what it wants.

28. Now, what energetic standpoint would you need to bring in what you want? Or, what beliefs are holding you back from being at peace with where you are?

29. If you were to teach a lesson on love to your friends and family, what points would you make?

30. How do you teach love?

31. For a purple, all emotions are acceptable. Describe how you have elicited emotional honesty in others in the past and helped them drop their walls, be real, and embrace the truth either in themselves or a situation where they received more love:

32. If you have ever felt suppressed or unacknowledged for your purple gift, write about that here. Why do you suppose that happened?

Purples can, at times, have strong emotional reactions to things people say and do. Having strong reactions to the way people are engaging or the way things look (or don't look) are two examples. (A purple friend once told me she was going to make all of her clothes from now on because she couldn't find anything to wear at Target. On another occasion she said she wanted to smash a person's iPhone because of lack of engagement.) Purples are looking for emotional depth from the things and people they encounter in the world, and actions that work against this understandably make them mad at times.

However, one of the reasons others set things up in the way that they do is because they have different spiritual gifts. They may not have meant to dress ugly, and for them, doing things without emotion or ignoring others may be a place they got stuck because they were focusing on something else (probably mental). Reflect on your experience with yourself and emotional reactions. How can you take things less personally in order to be more at peace with yourself and your experience?

33. How do you teach only love so that the people around you can learn what's really important?

34. Purples often do well when they have blue friends. The blue spiritual gift is the gift of the natural teacher. Blues help give purples some stability and structure. They are also able to talk to purples about what they can do with their knowledge, gifts, and life without making them feel judged. Because purples really want to avoid feeling

judged, purples feel good talking to blues. Also, purples have an innate respect for the teacher archetype. Read about the blue gift. Then, reflect on any reactions or thoughts you may have here:

35. Do you know any blues? How can you tell? What are the telling characteristics?

36. Describe what you have noticed about what it's like to interact with blues. What do they do for you? What can you do for them?

37. Now, review the observations about how purples and blues need each other in the Light Partners chapter.

    Purples and blues make good friends and colleagues and also ideal romantic partners due to this dynamic. What are some insights you have about this?

38. On the whole, how do you feel about being a purple? What is it like? What do you like the best about it? If you were to describe your gift to someone else, and let them know what it is like, what would you say?

39. Honoring your gift is very important. The more you honor it in yourself, the more others will honor it in you. The less likely you are to be walked on or your gifts disregarded. You will gain more respect for who you are and your light will shine brighter because these things will be present in you. In fact, they already are in a much deeper way, simply because you've engaged

this much with this information so far. What commitment are you willing to make regarding honoring yourself in the future?

40. How can you honor yourself for your own greatness?

41. Envision by drawing or writing what you will accomplish in the future with your gifts.

## Daily Practices

The following sequence of questions will help you notice your gifts more and how you share them. It will help you grow in your light, the light of who you are, and avoid pitfalls you may have or be experiencing on a large scale. One can continue this practice as long as one wishes as a helpful check and to raise awareness about living in giftedness—your special way of living in the light. The more aware you are, the more you will be able to avoid your traps and their associated consequences.

*Reflection on your soul-ray color:*

1. In what ways did you live out of your gift today? Be specific. (As a purple, you may consider how you went to blue or violet in addition to how you were dominantly in your own territory.)

2. Did you catch yourself going into any traps today? Were you able to avoid these traps?

3. Are you in a trap now and not aware of it? If so, what
   would you like to do about it? Make a commitment
   now. Either give yourself your gift right here and now, or
   make a decision to take action in this regard tomorrow.

The following list is a reminder of how to exit from the
purple trap. Because purples can shade blue or violet, once in
a while, a purple will get stuck in a trap of either of these two
colors. If you suspect this is happening, you may use the following list to remember how to remove yourself from the trap
of the other color in addition to your own.

*List of exits from purple's traps ...*

+ Use your intuition to tell you what is needed in a
  situation where you don't feel at your best.

+ Ask yourself what you need right now.

+ Give yourself wisdom and love (blue).

+ Know that God will give you everything you
  need, materially (purple).

+ Give yourself the gifts of mercy and compassion
  (violet).

## More Aspects of Your Gift

Now, let's talk more about that aspect of being a purple, which
is that purples can shade blue and violet in order to live out
their gifts. Reflect now on how, why, or when you shade blue

and violet. Read the description of blues in their giftedness and then answer the questions below.

1. When do you most often find yourself utilizing blue?

2. Could you expand this ability to serve a purpose?

While no one is a violet like a violet, purples can be very familiar with violet by close proximity (the 3rd eye and crown chakras are right next to each other.) Purples can also go to their violet to help others in a special way. Access to violet helps bring in the quality of unconditional love. Read the description of violets in their giftedness and reflect on how you feel violet at times.

1. When do you most often find yourself shading violet?

2. Could you expand this ability to serve a purpose?

## Meditation: God Giving You Everything You Need

This is a meditation to assist you in exiting from the purple traps. When you are in a trap, you can do this meditation to bring you into the light.

Sit with your feet flat on the floor with palms facing up on your lap.

Visualize a ball of grace (God's love) at the top of your head.

Breathe in grace, resting it on your heart. Exhale anything that is bothering or concerning you.

Breathe in grace, resting it on your heart, and letting it permeate your heart chakra and heart.

Breathe in grace one more time, exhaling any stuck emotions.

Imagine your crown chakra opening up like a flower.

Ask God to bring in the knowing and the feeling that God will provide all that is needed.

Ask that your entire being be saturated, every cell, with this knowing, this feeling.

Ask that you experience the trust, right here and now, that God provides everything needed for your well-being.

For several minutes, deeply feel this knowledge and this trust that God is providing all. Trust as deeply as possible for you right now (that is enough).

Now, contemplate what it is you need to do. Allow yourself to spend time with whatever comes up for you.

Now, bring in the quality of sincerity. Ask that you experience feeling sincere. Feel and know your sincerity, deeply.

You are contemplating with sincerity.

Do this until you get the answers you are looking for.
Ask and receive answers to anything you wish.

You are now at a place of greater peace. Better decisions
can now be made based on what happened for you in
meditation.

Feel free to modify this meditation to be as free flowing as you
wish. Do it as many times as you feel called to as you go throughout your week. Whenever you bring in the knowledge that God
will provide for you whatever you need, a space is opened up for
you to step out of the dark, into the light of your gift.

# 18

# Violet Workbook

### A Spiritual-Physical Spiritual Gift, Feminine in Nature: The Natural Helper

*You might be a violet if...*

+ You want to help people.

+ You see the goodness in people.

+ There are no barriers between you and them. You are sensitive to others' needs and feel interconnected with them.

+ You couldn't be yourself and wouldn't see the point of living if you didn't help people.

+ You commit to helping people on a regular basis to ensure divine intervention will occur through your presence and your love.

+ You love pure joy! You are so confident things will work out.

+ You can talk to a person exactly how they need to hear you and still get what you want.

+ You pave the way for miracles by doing many acts of kindness for others all the time.

+ You usually wish other people would be more courteous and aware of what's going on.

+ You frequently consider how other people will feel if something is said in a certain way, or if something happens.

+ You don't like to say things that other people would take the wrong way.

+ You feel impelled to include everyone, and notice right away if someone has been left out.

+ You know both sides of a conflict because you embody both sides. You bring the argument to a close on each side, independently, using arguments tailored for each.

+ You follow things to their natural order, helping things flow in the way they were meant to by nature and God or Goddess.

+ You often love other people as though they were your sister, brother, friend, or close relative.

+ You often want other people to succeed before you do. Or, you let them go first. This is how you provide for them.

+ Your ability to see people so well can be used to manipulate for your own gain, when your ego is in charge.

+ You're not afraid to sacrifice yourself for someone else, or a cause. Even when it costs you too much, you'll still defend doing so.

+ You are in touch with your feminine side. And proud of it.

+ You can fail to delegate your responsibilities because you're so committed to doing it all.

+ You sometimes can't grasp how wonderful your acts of kindness are.

+ You save people's feelings, putting the relationship first before most other concerns.

+ You follow the philosophy of Mitakuye Oyasin, the Lakota Sioux tradition of seeing everything as interconnected and related at all times, in all ways.

+ You know that everything is going to turn out according to the plan of your ultimate source light, and you will do anything to ensure that that happens.

### When in their giftedness, violets tend to ...
#### (According to Joseph Crane)

+ Be saints. Mother Teresa was undoubtedly a violet.

+ Be martyrs.

+ Serve—answering the phone; they would make good waitresses, butlers, stewards, volunteers, nurses, or people in human resources or childcare.

+ Be compassionate, tolerant, and tender, showing mercy.

+ Be attentive, making sure you have everything you need for what you are doing.

+ Give unconditional love to all.

+ Bring light and divine love.

+ Be joyful, confident, and faithful.

- Bring completion.

- Be manifesters of things from the spiritual to the physical.

- Be kind, gentle, and soft-spoken; their touch is that of a caress soothing the soul.

- Be spiritually connected with God beyond understanding.

- Just know everything is going to be okay.

- Prevent anything getting in their way when in service, like a mother tiger protecting her young.

- Be territorial and stand up for you as your personal champion, knowing you are perfect and holding you as such.

### When in their traps, violets tend to . . .
(According to Joseph Crane)

- Be a pain, not seeing the greatness they are. They can whine with the best of them.

- Refuse support, encouragement, or praise.

- Not get how wonderful they really are.

- Act out of a need to be acknowledged, praised, or rewarded rather than from a place of love.

+ Get overwhelmed and do too much for others to the neglect of themselves.

+ Allow themselves to be walked on and taken advantage of.

+ Not teach others how to get along.

+ Not take action when they see it's necessary.

## Reflection Questions

The following questions will help you reflect on your giftedness and where you tend to make mistakes. This will make you more conversant with your gift and better at deciding how to give it. What you learn will encourage you to add intention to your natural impulse to give.

While answering these questions, refer back to the information you just read about the gifts and traps as necessary.

1. You and your soul-ray color are both gifts, and as such, you have gifts to share with the world. This makes you a master, or expert, on how this gift is done. How do you see yourself living in your gifts?

2. Which aspects of your gift seem new to you? (Maybe you've never thought about them before.)

3. Which aspects of your gift would you like to embrace more fully now that you are consciously aware that you have special access to them? What would be the result?

4. What traps do you currently struggle with in your life? Traps are not "bad," however, may feel inconvenient or unpleasant. Traps occur when you are not "turned toward the light."

5. Can you identify triggers that move you into your traps? Write them here.

6. If you have ever felt suppressed or unacknowledged for your violet gift, write about that here. Why do you suppose that happened?

7. The way out of a trap for a violet is to give yourself the gift you give to others—mercy (kindness) and compassion. How would your life change if you did this often? (There is a mercy and compassion meditation at the end of this workbook to assist you in bringing in these qualities.)

8. Can you set a goal to become good at recognizing when you are in your gifts and when you are in your traps? How long do you think it would take? Which do you want to accomplish first?

9. What questions do you have about your gift?

10. Do you have any insights about what it is like to have this gift? No one knows your gift like you! Please share your insights below.

Violets sometimes do things for others just because they are good at helping. Some violets have always been perceived as the one who will do things, so they just go ahead and do them without really thinking about why or for whom. This can lead to being taken advantage of, feeling angry or resentful, and then not having any time for oneself. Doing too much is a trap, and so is doing something to gain recognition alone, rather than out of service.

Archangel Michael advises us to do things out of emotion, otherwise we go to sleep and sleepwalk through our day. Considering the kinds of things violets want to do, and what service they want to provide any organization, I encourage violets to be proactive about choosing whom they serve. Take some time to consider the questions below:

11. Who do you like to help, and why?

12. Who do you not like to help, and why? (It's okay to not want to help someone.)

13. If you were to do things for people either because it gave you joy or you chose to help someone who was serving the world—what would that look like? Who would you be helping, and how? Maybe the best help you can provide is through certain efforts, but not certain others—everyone has to prioritize, and it's okay for you to do that. If you need to prioritize who you help, do so now.

14. The Toleration List. Violets tend to get overwhelmed by doing too many activities, either in general, or specifically for others. Make a list of things that you cannot tolerate right now. Once you make this list, your conscious mind will become aware of these things, and you'll see yourself start to eliminate them (you can also set the intent to do so). You may update this list as often as you please, regularly crossing off the things you've succeeded in eliminating.

15. Can you delegate tasks to others? Make a list of all tasks you do regularly, either at home or at work, that either really do not need to be done or that someone else could do. Then, decide who to delegate them to, and do so. It's okay to ask for help! Other people can do things for a violet!

16. Remembering that there is no good, bad, right, or wrong, and knowing that traps are not "bad," take some time to think back on all the times when you may have over helped in the past. Ask yourself: was it worth it? Reflect on that question here. The angels have given me this question for violets to ask when they are in their traps or reflect on them.

17. Sometimes it can be hardest to actually receive our gift that we give, which in the case for violet, is helping others. The meditation on receiving support at the end of this workbook can help with this.

18. Violets often do well when they have red friends. The red spiritual gift is the gift of the natural leader. Reds help violets feel safe, grounded, and at peace. One reason for this is because reds have physical-physical energy, and thus, they are very grounded; they open up a place for violets to manifest into the physical world. Read about the red in the appendix, and then reflect on any reactions or thoughts you may have here.

19. Do you know any reds? How can you tell? What are the telling characteristics?

20. Describe what you have noticed about what it's like to interact with reds. What do they do for you? What can you do for them?

21. Now review the observations about how reds and violets need each other in the Light Partners chapter: How do you feel about reds and violets as reciprocal gifts?

22. In her book, *Color Your Life with Love*, Heidi Shelton Oliver reflects that violets need other violets because they themselves need that kind, caring, compassionate energy sometimes. Do you have a violet friend who cares for you? If not, can you be on the lookout for one?

23. Personally, how do you feel about being a violet? What is it like? What do you like the best about it? If you were to describe your gift to someone else, and let them know what it is like, what would you say?

24. Honoring your gift is very important. The more you honor it in yourself, the more others will honor it in you. The less likely you are to be walked on or your gifts disregarded. You will gain more respect for who you are and your light will shine brighter because these things will be present in you. In fact, they already are in a much deeper way, simply because you've engaged this much with this information so far. What commitment are you willing to make regarding honoring yourself in the future?

25. Violets are good at seeing others "greatness" and holding them in that light—sometimes to the surprise of those other people. Can you remember a time when you recently did this?

26. How can you honor yourself for your own greatness?

27. Envision by drawing or writing what it means to be a violet and what you will accomplish in the future with your gifts.

## Daily Practices

The following sequence of questions will help you notice your gifts more and how you share them. It will help you grow in your light, the light of who you are, and avoid pitfalls you may be experiencing on a large scale. One can continue this practice as long as one wishes, as a helpful check and to raise awareness about living in giftedness—your special way of living in the light. The more aware you are, the more you will be able to avoid your traps and their associated consequences.

*Reflection on your soul-ray color:*

1. In what ways did you live out of your gift today? Be specific. (As a violet, you may consider how you went to different colors to handle your gift, in addition to how you acted primarily as a violet from your space.) Please refer to the overview of the soul-ray colors when completing this section.

2. Did you catch yourself going into any traps today? Were you able to avoid these traps?

3. Are you in a trap now and not aware of it? If so, what would you like to do about it? Make a decision and a commitment now. Either give yourself your gift right here and now, or make a decision to take action in this regard tomorrow.

4. Memorize your gifts and traps.

The following list is a reminder of how to exit from the violet trap. Because violets can shade any other color to do their work, I have found that once in a while, a violet will get stuck in the trap of another color. If you suspect this is happening, you may use the list to remember how to remove yourself from the trap of the other color.

*List of exits from violet's traps ...*

+ Use your intuition to tell you what is needed in a situation where you don't feel at your best.

+ Ask yourself what you need right now.

+ Listen to what God is telling you and know the power you are (red).

+ Open your heart to the divine love you hold for others in joy (orange).

+ Connect to your natural knowing and ability to reason (yellow).

+ Give out of nothing save for the love of God (green).

+ Give yourself wisdom and love (blue).

+ Know that God will give you everything you need, materially (purple).

+ Give yourself the gifts of mercy and compassion (violet).

## More Aspects of Your Gift

Now, let's talk more about that aspect of being a violet, which is that violets can shade any of the soul-ray colors to do their jobs. I like to call violets "the rainbow," because more than any other gift, they live the rainbow and serve the rainbow. This may explain why you are "all over the place," or "good at so many things." Reflect now on how, why, or when you shade each color

of the rainbow. Read the description of each color in their giftedness and then answer the questions below.

1. When do you most often find yourself using another
   master chakra to do your gift? First answer for red,
   then for orange, green, blue, purple, and then violet.

2. If you need to be any of the colors, you can be. When
   might it be a good idea to mimic each one?

## Meditation on Mercy and Compassion

The following meditation will assist you in exiting from any of
the violet traps. Please use it to assist you when feeling overwhelmed, taken advantage of, or when you feel you are just
doing things out of a need to be acknowledged and not from a
place where you are serving causes that speak to you and are for
the greater good of the world. The angels have named the way
out of the trap—to give oneself mercy and compassion. I have
expanded this into a meditation and added, at the end, a way for
you to obtain direction from the space of clarity that the meditation gives you.

Sit with your feet flat on the floor, with palms facing
up, on your lap.

Visualize a ball of grace (God's love) at the top of your
head.

Breathe in grace, resting it on your heart. Exhale
anything that is bothering or concerning you.

Breathe in grace, resting it on your heart, letting it permeate your heart chakra and heart.

Breathe in grace one more time, exhaling any stuck emotions.

Imagine your crown chakra opening up like a flower.

Ask God to bring in the quality of mercy and let it saturate your entire being, every cell.

Deeply feel the quality of mercy (kindness) as it saturates your being. Remain here for several minutes, or as long as feels comfortable to you.

Let the mercy go wherever it needs to go in your body.

Now bring in the quality of compassion.

Feel compassion coming into your heart as the ray of energy that it is.

Ask that compassion saturate your entire being. Let it radiate to wherever it needs to go to help you.

It may go to the head, stay in the heart, move around your body. Let it.

Fill your being with compassion.

Now tap your forehead with your finger several times. Ask yourself what to do about the stressful or overwhelming situation (whatever is going on—regarding however you were showing up in your trap or your life as you sat down to do this meditation.)

Follow the instructions for greater peace!

Now you have brought yourself out of your trap, into a calm space, from which you can think and be free. You have asked your intuition what to do about your being in your trap, and received an answer. Do this as many times as you feel called to as you go throughout your day. You can also contemplate further on your own from this point in the meditation, about what to do. Whenever you bring in mercy and compassion, these qualities assist you in stepping into the light, out of the darkness of your traps.

## Moving Out of the Trap of Inaction

One way to stay in positive action in life (and this goes for any soul-ray) is to move into higher states of being, or states of joy, love, and freedom that raise your overall vibration. The first part of the process described helps you regain your energy; the second part helps you manage judging thoughts. It will eliminate your feeling negative.

Since violets can feel overwhelmed by the emotional needs of others, the second part of this process (having love come in) will help you recover your sense of self-worth. Violets often express the sentiment that they feel slimed by other people's energy and bogged down by their baggage. This meditation can help a violet clear that away and become clear about their own boundaries.

*Being Joy*

Tap into joy—remember a time when you felt joyful. Imagine concentric rings moving out from your heart center. See and feel the wave of joyful energy that goes out as a result.

Do something with this joy energy—be intentional.

If a contraction comes up, breathe into it, through it. Notice the negative. Without judging, simply notice. (This reforms thought patterns.)

*Being Love*

Feel the heart overflowing with love. Let the love fill your entire heart and field. Result: you don't feel judgment but have more confidence.

Notice any negative thing that comes up.

When feeling emotional around others, ask whether the emotion is yours or theirs.

If it's theirs, consciously let it go.

If it's yours, feel into it. (You can do this even if it's theirs; it will just leave faster if it's not yours.)

If it stays stuck, it's yours: you have a charge—feel the emotion through, completely.

When feeling blindsided by others, repeat steps above. Feel your emotion, take care of yourself first.

Tap into this—what asks to be said by spirit? Speak from kindness, firmly with confidence. Take action. It's okay to seek a compromise with others rather than bowing to what they want.

Remember, this brings you into the light, as inaction is a trap for violets when they notice people behaving poorly. (Violets help others learn how to get along.)

After you've said what you've said, feel any emotions that came up.

Once you've done this, you can move back into your expanded state, if you wish.

Notice anything negative, such as a negative state of mind.

Notice anything out of balance. Return yourself to balance however you feel called (i.e., I need to take a walk).

This protects you (it's divine protection). It disallows the other person from taking your mojo.

If all else fails, ask for divine help, intervention, and protection. Know 100 percent that it will show up.

Bless the heart of the other person. This protects you with grace and keeps the other person's negativity from affecting you. If necessary, you can repeat "bless your heart, bless your heart, bless your heart" toward the person silently, and when muscle tested, you will see that you will not be affected by any negative thoughts they may be having about you.

## Meditation to Open Heart to Receptivity

This process helps you practice receptivity and receiving support. Both are key for violets, who can have a hard time opening themselves to receive their own gift. This is very important for you to be able to live in balance.

Imagine a ball of grace (God's love) at your crown chakra.

Breathe in, bringing the grace down to rest it on your heart. Breathe out any thoughts that are not serving you.

Breathe in grace, resting it on your heart; breathe out any fears.

Breathe in grace, resting it on your heart; breathe out any remaining negative thoughts.

Imagine a tiny light in your heart. Watch it, see it grow. Allow the light to grow and grow. This is the light of source. As it grows and gets bigger and bigger, the heart expands. Allow the heart to expand.

Inhale, exhale. Get comfortable.

Now visualize two wooden doors on your heart, opening in. Let the doors open in.

Let them open in as much as they want to. Breathe in.

Breathe though any contractions you feel. If the doors want to close, let them close. Then simply breathe in and out again, several times.

Imagine the doors opening again when you are ready. Just breathe into any tightness, and breathe out. It's natural to feel contraction and expansion. Breathe into the contractions, and your doors open more.

Let the doors open in, and you feel receptive.

In that place of receptivity, stay and imagine what it is you want to receive.

Visualize yourself receiving the support of others, allowing them to come into your life and be of service to you, either emotionally, physically, spiritually, or mentally—in any way you want to receive support at this time.

Do this for three to five minutes.

Feel your receptivity and become comfortable with "receptive mode."

You may remain in receptive mode as long as you would like to, continuing to meditate. Remember, in order for someone to give, there must be someone to receive. The angels have said, "Receive, that others may receive when you give." Receiving and giving are two halves of a whole that creates balance.

If any variations to the above meditation come to you, feel free to flow with them and integrate them to personalize this process.

If you want to shift the energies, proactively, you can; simply see and feel the energies becoming what you want them to be. You may imagine what you do want to see happen as you did in the above heart receptivity meditation, and see and feel yourself in that experience. Be sure to bring the qualities to the experience that you desire to have, for example, "a loving relationship" rather than "a relationship."

# Conclusion

Each master chakra is unique. You have a master chakra, and you can choose to focus your gifts from a place of love and trust in your spiritual connectedness. I know from experience that doing the work it takes to use well the gifted traits of your master chakra will help you get a leg up if you are stranded. It will change your life if you do the work to live in your gifted areas, however you can figure out how to do that. It's like a bootstrap, and there are few of those floating around.

Knowing how to recognize the spiritual gifts in people lets you understand them faster and more fully. It helps you judge character. Knowing and honoring people's gifts help you respect and love them more, and handle them better. This, in turn, lets you live a better, cleaner, happier existence with them. It lets you choose who you let into your life with more confidence. That's why you need awareness not only of your own gift, but also of its traps and of the traps of others. You need knowledge of all the spiritual gifts, not just your own.

Remember, you don't have to play every role for every person, all the time. You don't have to be all the chakras—you get to be one chakra. And no one needs to be everything for you (unless they are a violet). Honoring a person's master chakra can help you relate to both their gifts and traps. It can also help you to use your own chakras better and develop them, even if they are not your masters. We still need to use the yellow gift, even if we are not yellow. But we can learn from our blue teachers how to have better communication and from our purple friends how to love. This makes our other chakras stronger.

All of the spiritual gifts, or colors, are important and valuable. Each one deepens our understanding of our existence. As partners on our journey in this world, the colors we are not bring us what we need. In turn, we bring something to others that they do not have. The aspect of the spectrum that we live out, or the light that we filter, helps us focus and hone in on one thing humanity needs, and needs often. We become masters of one trade. When we truly get what that is, we can emerge into the highest expression of our being—both for ourselves and for others. This is not the first or the last pathway toward enlightenment, it is but one that works like a charm.

# Appendix:
## Collected Characteristics of Each Master Chakra

If you would like to draw on the energy of your master chakra more intensely, then try wearing the color of your chakra on the day of the week where its vibration comes into the planet more strongly. The master chakra days are listed below. You can also view each day as an opportunity to get a special leg up on the concerns handled by the master chakra of that day. Just jump into that master chakra's energy by doing what you need to do, which matches what they do, on that day. Each day of the week supports the vibration of a different energy mode. A person can get more of their master chakra work done on the day correlated to that chakra. Or, they can consider it a day of rest.

*Wearing Your Chakra Color*

+ **Monday:** Orange … time to have fun.

+ **Tuesday:** Yellow … good for researching your upcoming decisions.

+ **Wednesday:** Green … good for bringing checkbooks, health, relationships, and anything into balance.

+ **Thursday:** Blue … good for boning up on knowledge and giving from your heart.

+ **Friday:** Purple … good for emotional expression and doing romantic things for others.

+ **Saturday:** Violet … keep up with your chores, adding random acts of kindness into the mix.

+ **Sunday:** Red … plan your week around your goals, and start something now.

I am sure you can think of many more things to do on each one of these days that matches up with its concomitant master chakra concerns. It's limitless, boundless, and creative in nature how you use these days. Don't forget about you, though. Honor yourself, and all will be well.

## Enhancing Your Spiritual Gifts Through Crystals

A handful of crystals vibrate in harmony with each spiritual gift's interplay with its appropriate chakra color. These crystals enhance the connection of the person with whatever chakra they wish to combine with when doing their work in the world. It entails more than just getting a chakra into proper alignment without regard for anything else. These crystals can help you connect with your own gift or a different color-gift. You may want to carry the appropriate crystal to support what you are doing. It helps you attract more of that color's vibration into your life. It helps you use the gift of that master chakra even if it is not your own. While carrying your own crystal, let it be a reminder to you of who you are when you are in your best self. You can use your own crystals to manifest with, because they negate vibrations that are not of you or your gift. They can increase the wherewithal and stamina you bring to carrying out your intention. They increase your intentions' effectiveness. The crystals are recommended in the order in which I feel they are most effective. The list of crystals is provided by Joseph Crane.

+ **Red:** ruby

+ **Orange:** carnelian and orange sapphire

+ **Yellow:** orange calcite (which is a deeper form of yellow than yellow calcite) and yellow sapphire

+ **Green:** green fluorite, green kyanite, and emerald

+ **Blue:** blue azurite, blue aventurine, blue sapphire

+ **Purple:** amethyst and benitoite

+ **Violet:** charoite, violet calcite, and lavender jade

## Key Characteristics of Each Master Chakra

*Motives:*

+ **Red:** To lead, especially groups, to a specific goal or to greater, gigantic purpose.

+ **Orange:** To promote, to make others happy, uplifting them, and to provide counsel to them when the chips are down.

+ **Yellow:** To think, to research, and to seek truth. To put details into a whole. To know naturally and share that knowing.

+ **Green:** To heal, to fix, and bring everything into balance. To love with compassion and be strong.

+ **Blue:** To educate others and bring them into alignment with God.

+ **Purple:** To portray life lessons through art, to teach love, and to create beauty.

+ **Violet:** To serve others and show them kindness and compassion.

*Concerns About Other People:*

+ **Red:** What you are doing in this moment, and how effective it is. Whether you're engaging in your life purpose. Where you are at in general.

+ **Orange:** Whether you are happy and healthy. Whether you experience enjoyment in life. How much fun you are having.

+ **Yellow:** How the paths that you follow lead you and where they lead you. Whether you know the facts and also discovered the truth at the same time. What your foundation for your life is.

+ **Green:** Whether you have the money, energy, or the clarity you need. Whether you are in or out of balance on a given day. How perfectly your body, mind, and spirit function together.

+ **Blue:** How you learn and grow. If you create expansion for yourself and others. What your knowledge develops into.

+ **Purple:** Your emotional awareness and acumen. Your emotional honesty level. Your deep emotions of most kinds. Whether you love others and how so. Your creativity and its application for life.

+ **Violet:** Your expressions of kindness. Living up to your own greatness.

*Questions this color evaluates and then addresses through the giving of its gift:*

+ **Red:** Are you in action? What actions are you taking to achieve results? What are the results?

What's the bottom line you need to reach?
Do you stay in the present moment? Are you
grounded? Are you safe?

+ **Orange:** Do you have a sense of humor? Do you
go with the flow? Are you in touch with your
emotions? Can you find the silver lining in your
experiences? What did you learn from your
experiences? Do you feel joy on a regular basis?
Do you see the divine light in others?

+ **Yellow:** Are you paying attention to the details?
Have you found out the truth, either through
research and analysis or some other way? How
much do you believe what you are told, or even
what you read, versus thinking for yourself? Have
you based your actions on a foundation of truth?
How precise are you?

+ **Green:** Does the structure of your life work
for you? Do your habits lead you in or out of
balance? Do you have access to processes and
ways of doing things that make for healthy body,
mind, and spirit? Have you found peace? Do you
maintain calm in all situations?

+ **Blue:** Are you moving forward rapidly? Do you
have the knowledge you need, which is power,
and would set you free? Do you focus on body,

mind, emotion, and spirit, without neglecting one for another? Do you speak your truth? Do you connect choice with consequence? Do you know how to make connections and use them for your greater benefit?

+ **Purple:** How much love do you experience in your relationships? Do you allow yourself to be creative? Do you manifest what you desire effectively? Do you create beauty, for all to see, even if it's only through your clothing style? Do you express yourself artistically? Do you prioritize love? Do you have fun?

+ **Violet:** Do you create a loving, harmonious environment around you? Do you express compassion and love to others and yourself? Are you spiritually rich? Do you help other people? Do you enrich their lives? Do you think about the impact your actions will have on others before you act? Are you courteous and kind?

### Shows up in the world as:

+ **Red:** Physical-physical

+ **Orange:** Physical-emotional

+ **Yellow:** Physical-mental

+ **Green:** Spiritual-spiritual

+ **Blue:** Spiritual-mental

+ **Purple:** Spiritual-emotional

+ **Violet:** Spiritual-physical

*Example tools of the trade, or the items that might appear on this color's workbench. Some are intangible:*

+ **Red:** Emergency equipment, such as a first aid kit, a parachute, a rope. A wand, a laser pointer, a pointed finger. A whiteboard to draw up plans. To do lists for other people. A clean slate.

+ **Orange:** Smiley face stickers, jokes, cameras, party items, colorful clothing, bubbles, mirror ball.

+ **Yellow:** Books of all categories, computer to access the internet, nature, cycles, inventions and equipment to make them, items in collections, and compiled information: flash drives, notebooks, papers, etc.

+ **Green:** Money, process, healing awareness, a crowbar, knife, scissors and tape, dishrag, dust-rag, vacuum, how-to manuals, magic, and containers for separating the negative and un-serving from the pure of heart.

+ **Blue:** Books. A crystal grid used to read the connections between everyone, the internet of time and motion, a clipboard for keeping track of all those they are currently in the act of molding, strategies for teaching and learning, and student papers and love letters.

+ **Purple:** Well-adjusted behaviors, collected art, barely started art, stylish clothing, creative spaces, paint, paint-brushes, colored pencils with pens, a romantic relationship, Christmas lights and other décor in abundance, organized clutter, seize-the-day attitude, music.

+ **Violet:** Books on etiquette and human disgruntlement, cute art, a structure of thought that includes morality, aprons, medicine, matches, tissues, meaningful items with sentiment attached, housework, wedding ring, and relationships of all kinds.

*Fitting titles:*

+ **Red:** Boss, coach, entrepreneur

+ **Orange:** Life of the party, ace-in-the hole, salesperson

+ **Yellow:** Father to all, mapmaker, philosopher, thinker

+ **Green:** Healer, fixer, mechanic, doctor

+ **Blue:** Brother to all, teacher, advisor, sage, judge

+ **Purple:** Artist, priest(ess) of love, Michelangelo, magician, goddess

+ **Violet:** Mother to all, secretary, nurse, concierge, saint

## Roles played when traps are at an extreme:

+ **Red:** Bully, dictator

+ **Orange:** Swindler

+ **Yellow:** Stalker, sociopath

+ **Green:** Pessimist, scrooge

+ **Blue:** Thug

+ **Purple:** Con artist

+ **Violet:** Martyr

## Level of reliance on others for self-esteem and spiritual work tasks:

+ **Red:** Independent

+ **Orange:** Independent

+ **Yellow:** Independent

+ **Green:** Interdependent

+ **Blue:** Interdependent

+ **Purple:** Interdependent

+ **Violet:** Interdependent

*Spiritual gift gender, or chakra gender:*
+ **Red:** Feminine

+ **Orange:** Feminine

+ **Yellow:** Masculine

+ **Green:** Masculine

+ **Blue:** Masculine

+ **Purple:** Masculine

+ **Violet:** Feminine

*Gradation of gender trait and balance:*
+ **Red:** Masculine-feminine—this feminine gift has a masculine quality.

+ **Orange:** Feminine-masculine—this feminine gift has a preponderance of feminine traits.

+ **Yellow:** Masculine- feminine—this masculine gift seems masculine, matched later by its feminine side.

+ **Green:** Masculine-feminine—this masculine gift presents as masculine. It has a preponderance of masculine traits.

+ **Blue:** Masculine-feminine—in this gift, the masculine goes first but is closely balanced by its feminine traits.

- **Purple:** Feminine-masculine—this masculine gift has an abundance of feminine traits.

- **Violet:** Feminine-Masculine—this feminine gift has the most feminine qualities of any other.

*Side chakras:*

- **Red:** Orange and violet

- **Orange:** Red and yellow

- **Yellow:** Orange and green

- **Green:** Yellow and blue

- **Blue:** Green and purple

- **Purple:** Blue and violet

- **Violet:** Purple and red

*Light partners—friends and colleagues:*

- **Red:** Red and violet

- **Orange:** Yellow, blue, and purple

- **Yellow:** Orange and green

- **Green:** Yellow and blue

- **Blue:** Orange and green

- **Purple:** Orange

- **Violet:** Red and violet

*Reciprocal colors: equal partners that are mutually beneficial for the world:*

+ **Red:** Red and violet

+ **Orange:** Orange and orange

+ **Yellow:** Yellow and green

+ **Green:** Green and yellow

+ **Blue:** Blue and purple

+ **Purple:** Purple and blue

+ **Violet:** Violet and red